Crossing to Talikota

Crossing to Talikota

Girish Karnad

OXFORD
UNIVERSITY PRESS

Oxford University Press is a department of the University of Oxford. It furthers the University's objective of excellence in research, scholarship, and education by publishing worldwide. Oxford is a registered trademark of Oxford University Press in the UK and in certain other countries.

Published in India
by Oxford University Press
2/11 Ground Floor, Ansari Road, Daryaganj, New Delhi 110 002, India

First Edition published in 2019

ISBN-13 (print edition): 978-0-19-949615-0
ISBN-10 (print edition): 0-19-949615-3

ISBN-13 (eBook): 978-0-19-909825-5
ISBN-10 (eBook): 0-19-909825-5

Typeset in Minion Pro 10.5/14
by The Digiultrabooks Pvt. Ltd., New Delhi 110 096
Printed in India by Thomson Press India Ltd.

For
Professor Richard M. Eaton
University of Arizona, Tucson
who led me to 'Aliya' Ramaraya

CONTENTS

PREFACE

When one looks at the history of the Deccan during the last millennium, three events stand out, not only for their importance for the region, but for the impact they have had on the political and cultural map of the whole of India: the revolution created by the Lingayat poet-philosophers under Basavanna and the Vacanakaras in the twelfth century, the spectacular achievements of the Vijayanagara Empire four centuries later, and the reign of Tipu Sultan, which was the last assertion of national pride against colonial onslaught. All three ended catastrophically but left legacies that continue to shape national life and thought even today. I have already dealt with these events in *Tale-Danda* and *The Dreams of Tipu Sultan*. Here is my attempt to understand the third one, Vijayanagara, which despite being one of the most powerful military edifices of its age, collapsed overnight after a single battle.

Ironically, despite the massive scale and impact of the battle, its location has never been precisely identified. Talikota has generally been accepted as the village near which the two armies clashed. However, the twin villages of Rakkasagi and Tangadagi, referred to in some contemporary documents as Rakshasa–Tangadi, also have a plausible claim. I am fascinated by the contradiction implicit in the combination of the Sanskrit word 'Rakshasa' (demon) with the Urdu word 'Tangadi' (shank) and, therefore, have used that name as the title for the Kannada version of this play.

The first historian to draw attention to the Vijayanagara era was Robert Sewell in his pioneering work, *A Forgotten Empire* (1900). His colonialist interpretation—that simple religious antagonism was at the base of the conflict—has deeply influenced, and continues to shape, subsequent academic studies, although research since then has shown how simplistic and reductionist Sewell's understanding of the situation was.

It is also to Sewell that we owe the mistaken belief that the empire was called 'Vijayanagara'. In fact, it was called 'Karnataka', as Sewell himself admits, the name 'Vijayanagara' signifying only the capital, and 'Hampi' the sacral core of the city. Sewell initiated and popularized the usage 'Vijayanagara' for the entire empire to involve Telugu scholars in his research, and even Kannada scholars accepted his lead. I have followed the practice in this play as the theatre is not a place to correct academic errors.

It should be noted that the family of Ramaraya spoke Telugu although the official language of the empire was Kannada.

Sanskrit and Kannada words such as 'Nagara' get truncated to 'Nagar' in Persian and non-Dravidian Indian pronunciation. I have spelt the names using both spelling variations in the text to reflect this difference in pronunciation between the Dravidian-language–speaking characters and the non-Dravidian-language–speaking characters.

Resonant in its political and social implications is the neologism *Suratrana* (the power of gods), the Sanskritized form of 'Sultan', which the ruling elite of Vijayanagara adopted as part of their proud title. This title, which was used in different combinations over 250 years, is evidence of how the ruling class attempted 'to bolster its international standing by Islamicizing the culture of its court', according to Wagoner.

It was the Kannada critic Kirtinath Kurtkoti who first drew my attention to the seminal role played by 'Aliya' (son-in-law) Ramaraya in the relentless build-up to the cataclysm of 1565. However, it was Richard M. Eaton's essay on him in *A Social History of the Deccan, 1300–1761* that awakened me to the tragic dimensions of this exceptional figure, who was the absolute ruler of the empire without being accepted as its head. The book Eaton later wrote with Phillip Wagoner, *Power, Memory, Architecture, 1300–1600*, further illuminated my understanding of the forces that shaped the era. My play contains much that I have borrowed from these two books.

Having such friends as John Fritz and George Michell, who have spent a lifetime working on Hampi, has helped me visualize the city not as an archaeological site but as a living organism.

Fortunately for me, during the last few years, the F. G. Halakatti Research Centre, Vijayapura, has published eighteen volumes of documents dating from the Adil Shahi regime in Kannada translation under the directorial supervision of Dr Krishna Kolhar Kulkarni. Thanks to the sudden availability of this invaluable material, it was possible for me to have direct access to the content, if not the language, of the Bijapur historians Firishta and Shirazi. Dr Kolhar Kulkarni also personally guided me to other texts and information which I did not even know existed but which enabled me to make the play more 'full-blooded'.

My thanks are also due to Professor C. M. Naim, Dr Najaf Haidar, and Zafer Mohiuddin for their guidance on many of the details of mediaeval Islamic culture.

As this text goes to press, the Sight and Sound Performing Arts has announced that the world premiere of the play will be performed on 2 October 2019 at Chowdayya Memorial Hall, Bengaluru. It will be directed by Arjun Sajnani, who had earlier directed my plays *Bali* and *The Fire and the Rain* with success. The production is supported by Rohini Nilekani Philanthropies and Nandan Nilekani, with music by Ambi Subramaniam and production design by Shama Zaidi.

What more can a playwright ask for?

Girish Karnad
19 April 2019

DRAMATIS PERSONAE

'ALIYA' RAMARAYA	the ruler of Vijayanagara
VENKATADRI	Ramaraya's younger brother
TIRUMALA RAYA	Ramaraya's younger brother
SADASHIVA RAYA	puppet emperor of Vijayanagara
TIRUMALAMBA	Ramaraya's mother
SATYABHAMA	Ramaraya's wife, Sadashiva's cousin
HUSSAIN NIZAM SHAH	Sultan of Ahmadnagar
ALI ADIL SHAH	Sultan of Bijapur
ALI BARID SHAH	Sultan of Bidar
IBRAHIM QUTB SHAH	Sultan of Golconda
HAKIM QASIM BEG	Nizam Shah's medical attendant
BEGUM HUMAYUN SULTANA	Nizam Shah's wife

Rumi Khan, Bisalappa Nayaka, Narasimha,
courtiers, citizens, maids, soldiers, heralds, and so on.

PROLOGUE

SCENE ONE

Vijayanagara, 1565

The landscape surrounding the city is of rolling hills, elephantine boulders, valleys, and caverns. It's a starlit night. The stage presents a silent, almost lunar, landscape.

A couple of men step out stealthily from behind the boulders, carrying bundles and weapons, and peer around. It is evident from their attire—turbans, pyjamas, and belts with weapons— that they are foreign soldiers. They take a few steps, listen, and dive behind the rocks and wait.

A longish silence. A group of men, distinctly civilian, again clutching bundles, emerge cautiously round the corner, looking over their shoulders in fear. They are aware of the possibility of attack from any side and keep their weapons within reach. They are nevertheless not prepared when the soldiers pounce on them and pin a couple of them to the ground. A scuffle ensues. Some of the civilians escape but the soldiers manage to capture a couple of them.

CIVILIAN ONE: Don't kill us. Please. Don't. Spare us.

SOLDIER ONE: Where are you going? Can you understand me?

CIVILIAN TWO: Yes, yes. I can speak your tongue. A little.

SOLDIER ONE: Where are you going?

CIVILIAN ONE: Food. A bite. Water. We are starving.

SOLDIER TWO: At this time of the night?

CIVILIAN TWO: Soldiers during the day. Robbers. Murderers.

SOLDIER ONE: Where do you live? Where have you come from?

CIVILIAN ONE: Here. In these rocks. Caves. There's no other place.

CIVILIAN TWO: Our houses are gone. Burnt down. Decimated. Foreign soldiers everywhere. And bandits.

SOLDIER TWO: Where's your family?

(*No reply.*)

Come on. If you try to—

CIVILIAN TWO: I'll tell you. I'll tell you. Don't kill us. Please. We fall at your feet. We have sent them to our village.

SOLDIER ONE: What're you doing here in this wasteland with your family away?

SOLDIER TWO: If you tell lies—

(*Pushes the civilian to the floor and presses his sword on his neck.*)

CIVILIAN TWO: Have mercy. We aren't lying. It's the truth.

CIVILIAN ONE: Why kill us? We've nothing with us. Not a cowrie.

SOLDIER ONE: Show us where you've hidden your family. Wife, children. Where are they?

CIVILIAN ONE: We've nothing with us. Our houses were burnt down to ashes. They even dug up the foundations to look for hidden fortunes. We live like jackals. Foraging at night.

SOLDIER ONE: We don't believe a word of yours. All that gold and silver which you looted—where's it all hidden?

CIVILIAN TWO: Oh God in Heaven! We saw nothing of it. Mobs fell on the city and ransacked. We are left here with nowhere to go.

SOLDIER ONE: Show us where you've managed to store all that you have collected so far. Where have you stashed it?

CIVILIAN TWO: Why threaten us now, sir? What's the use? You should've come the moment the battle was over. The entire city was looted in a matter of days. Right in front of our eyes. Palaces. Temples. Reduced to ashes.

CIVILIAN ONE: Buried treasures dug up. Gold, jewellery. Coffers of the traders and merchants ripped up. Non-stop. You should've been here then.

SOLDIER ONE (*to Soldier Two*): All those stories about the city. Its limitless riches. We never thought they would make such a quick job of it.

SOLDIER TWO: I told you we had to rush. We missed most of it. Curse our luck!

CIVILIAN ONE: And the bloodshed. The looters went berserk. We couldn't even leave the city. We had to find shelter in these rocks. Didn't even dare peep out. We know nothing, sir.

CIVILIAN TWO: We don't know where to find the next mouthful.

CIVILIAN ONE (*to Civilian Two*): I told you we shouldn't move out tonight. It's too bright.

(*Weeps.*)

SOLDIER ONE: Shut up or we'll finish you off.

CIVILIAN TWO: No, no, please. He's my father. He knows the paths here. If you kill him we are stuck here forever—in this maze. We'll never get back. Please.

SOLDIER ONE: Where do you live in these rocks? Show us.

CIVILIAN TWO: There're caverns here. Deep underground passages. They run for miles. We hide in them. Like rats.

SOLDIER TWO: And you have hidden your wealth there?

CIVILIAN ONE: Wealth? What wealth? There was nothing left to take.

SOLDIER ONE: All right. Take us to your cave. Let's check for ourselves what you've got there. Go on. Lead us. Lead.

CIVILIAN TWO: It's quite far. You'll have to crawl. Slither like mongooses.

SOLDIER ONE: Tie him up. Lead us. Move.

(*Their hands are tied.*)

Now tell us. Who did the looting? Were they soldiers from the battlefield? Local goons? Who?

CIVILIAN ONE: No difference. They all fell on us—like wild beasts, like demons.

SOLDIER ONE: Is it true the members of the palace are also hiding here? The princes—the royal family?

CIVILIAN TWO: Don't know. Wouldn't recognize them even if we saw them. Haven't seen any ever.

SOLDIER TWO: They say Ramaraya's son too is here with his family. All that wealth! Gold—silver—precious stones. Where's it gone? They couldn't have moved it all out too far.

CIVILIAN ONE: They took out the treasures on loaded elephants. Hundreds of them. And women and children. We'd problems enough of our own.

SOLDIER ONE: Move on. Don't try to trick us.

(*After they pass a few boulders Civilian One whistles softly. A woman peeps out, sees the soldiers, and rushes back into the cave. Soldier One follows her, grabs her, and pulls her out.*)

SOLDIER ONE: Don't try to raise an alarm. We'll cut you to pieces. What do you have here in these bundles? Untie them.

(*Tears open some bundles. Searches around. While his attention is straying, the woman picks up a long metal stick and hits him on his head. When the other soldier, taken by surprise, turns to his companion, the young companion slips the rope with which his wrists are tied round his neck and throttles him. The woman picks up a rock and smashes the soldier's skull. The killings are fairly expertly done.*

They push the two dead bodies to the ground and start rifling through their clothes.

A child bawls out inside the cave. The woman runs in. The civilian inspects the soldier's sword.)

CIVILIAN TWO: Good steel. Probably from Damascus.

(*Unties the hands of the older man.*)

We'll dispose of them in the ravine tomorrow morning. Let's go. Must find out what they were carrying. They must've looted others before us. Hidden the stuff where we ran into them. Come—where they surprised us—before other bastards stumble on to it.

(*They depart while the woman pats the child to sleep.*)

SCENE TWO

The Palace Gates

Midnight. It's a dark night lit by torches and standing lamps. Suddenly there is a clatter of horse hooves, shouting. The gates are banged.

VOICE: Open the gates! Open the gates!

GATEKEEPERS: No orders to open the gates at night. Come back in the morning.

VOICE: Open the gates! Orders from the Commander-in-Chief!

GATEKEEPERS: Don't talk rot. Go away! Commander-in-Chief? He's at the front.

(*The voices multiply and become more insistent and panic-stricken. A group of guards reluctantly opens the gates.*)

GUARDS: Who're you? What's happening here? Don't you know the palace rules?

SOLDIER: We've come from Tirumala Raya. The Chief. He's on his way.

GUARD: What're you burbling? Tirumala Raya's in Talikota. On the battlefield. Don't you know? If he's here, where're his bodyguards?

SOLDIER: Oh God! It's a calamity. The skies have collapsed on us. We've lost the battle. It's a rout!

GUARDS: That's impossible.

SOLDIER ONE: A bloodbath. We're done for! Finished! Our army's running scared.

GUARDS: Not possible. We, lose?

(*The commotion is now spreading. It's not clear what's going on.*)

SOLDIER TWO: An arrow pierced Tirumala Raya's eye. He's fled from the front with his men. He's on his way back here.

GUARD: God forbid. And where's the Master?

SOLDIER THREE: What about Bisalappa Nayaka? And Vengala Nayaka? Where are their men?

SOLDIER THREE: God alone knows. Probably fleeing back to their villages.

SOLDIER FOUR (*freshly arrived*): Open the inner portals! Tirumala Raya's orders. Hurry up! Vacate the palace. Wake up Emperor Sadashiva Raya. We've to get him out of the palace. Right away!

GUARD: His Imperial Majesty cannot be disturbed. Orders—

SOLDIER FOUR: Shut up, you fool. Listen to us. We've rushed down from Talikota—direct. Haven't even paused to water our horses. It's the doomsday. Disaster. Summon the entire palace staff. The orders are to get the Imperial Majesty Sadashiva Raya out, ready to leave. Summon the mahouts. Inform the ladies. Hurry up!

(*Panic-stricken voices spread across the background. Screams for help and shouts envelope the whole city.*)

The Elephant Stables

NARASIMHA: Mahadevappa! Mahadevappa! Where the hell's that swine? Get the mahouts up. Instantly! How many elephants are there in the stables? Round up all the mahouts at hand. Instantly.

GUARD ONE: Now? Most of the mahouts are at the battlefront. Only the oldies are here. And those who're unwell.

NARASIMHA: Kick them up. Orders from Tirumala Raya, the Commander-in-Chief! How many elephants are immediately available in the stables? Get them all out and to the palace yards.

GUARD ONE: Perhaps a thousand. Not more than fifteen hundred, I don't think.

NARASIMHA: Get them all ready to move out. Rush them to the palace. Put every mahout on duty. Look sharp.

GUARD ONE: Is what we heard true? The watchmen were shouting—

NARASIMHA: It's a catastrophe. We've lost the battle—our army's in shambles. Oh God! Hurry up! Get all the elephants to the palace yards. Bring out all the women and children from the royal quarters. The royal dependants, the servants, the other residences. The lot. They've to leave for Penukonda.

(*A guard comes running in.*)

GUARD TWO: There's rioting going on in the city, sir. Mobs are on the rampage, looting. It only took the news from Talikota to be whispered and the marketplaces began to be ransacked. It's mayhem.

GUARD ONE: They're attacking the temples. Oh God! Oh God!

GUARD TWO: Who are they? Citizens? Our own people? The riff-raff?

(*The cacophony gets shriller, more widespread. In the background, buildings go up in flames.*)

GUARDS ONE: Can't see in the dark, sir. But all the gold and silver in the goldsmith's quarters is being heaped out into the streets. Mounds of it. Gold, diamonds, precious stones—they're not even killing each other for it. There's so much to grab. Jewellery, gold, silk. Precious stones. Heaped on the pavements.

The Ladies' Quarters

EUNUCH: Madam! Madam! There are soldiers at the main door. They want to be let in.

(*Maids rush in, followed by Satyabhama, Ramaraya's wife.*)

MAIDS (*weeping and wailing*): Madam, they say they are from the battlefront. What's happening? What're we to do?

SATYABHAMA: And where are the palace guards? What's all this shouting and screaming about? Disturbing the ladies' quarters at this hour? Are there no guards here?

EUNUCH: It's bad news from the front, madam. Not just bad. Terrible. Chief Tirumala Raya's in the front yard.

SATYABHAMA: Brother-in-Law? What's he doing here? Let him in. Let him. May God protect us from all evil. Where's he? What's he waiting for?

(*Tirumala Raya stumbles in supported by a helper. A bandage covers one of his eyes, but blood can be seen trickling down his cheeks.*)

Brother-in-Law, what're you doing here? Where's the Master?

TIRUMALA (*collapsing to the floor*): Oh God! What can I say, sister-in-law? It's *pralaya*—end of the world! The worst calamity one could imagine—Ayyo!—How can I talk about it?—With what tongue?

(*Starts hitting himself on the forehead with his fists, weeping. More residents of the ladies' quarters rush out from inside. They are panic-stricken seeing Tirumala Raya's state, and cling to each other, crying.*)

SATYABHAMA (*shouting*): Stop breast-beating. No wailing, please. Please. Stop screaming. Tell us what's happened.

TIRUMALA: The worst of fates, Sister-in-Law. The unthinkable.

SATYABHAMA: Enough. I said, enough. Tell us the worst. Where's the Master?

TIRUMALA: The battle's gone badly for us. Our army's been put to rout. There's terrible bloodshed on the battlefield—it's the end of the world. And Brother was swept into the chaos. Before anyone could do anything—we lost sight of him.

SATYABHAMA: What do you mean? Is he all right? Tell me that. Is he safe?

TIRUMALA: We've become orphans, Sister-in-Law. Bereft of a roof—of protection. Why, oh why am I chosen to bring you this news?

SATYABHAMA (*to the other women*): Shut up. Shut up. I'll have you whipped if you don't shut up. You are a disgrace to the royal family. (*To Tirumala*) But was there no one else with him—looking after him?

TIRUMALA: He was surrounded by guards. But he wouldn't listen to anyone. He rushed out on his own.

SATYABHAMA: And where was Brother-in-Law Venkatadri? Where were you?

TIRUMALA: We were all caught in the melee. Venkatadri has also vanished. Cursed am I that I've to give you these evil tidings, cursed for the next seven lives. Spit on me.

SATYABHAMA: Perhaps the Master has been taken prisoner. Then perhaps he'll be safe. After all, we have let the Sultans go free in the past. We haven't harmed them. Where's Adil Shah? Yes. Have you asked him?

EUNUCH: The Queen Mother's here.

(*Tirumalamba is brought in on a litter. She is nearly a hundred and senile, with an ability to spark into life suddenly. The wailing goes down upon her arrival.*)

TIRUMALAMBA: Who's it, Satyabhama? Is it Tirumala? When did you come, son? Where's Ramaraya?

TIRUMALA: What can I say, Amma? I wanted my tongue to rot before I uttered—

(*She gives him a frozen stare, unwilling to digest the shock. Then gently*)

TIRUMALAMBA: Hush, now. In the last fifty years, my son has never stepped in here without first taking my *arati* and blessings. He always insists on bringing me the news of victory himself. He will come. He'll give me the news himself. Ramaraya must be waiting outside. Send him in. Satyabhama, you know how to receive your husband. Tell the maids to decorate the *chandrashala*. Flowers. Pearls. And the musicians—yes, send for them. And the Head Priest.

(*She signals to the litter-bearers who take her in. Satyabhama turns to go.*)

TIRUMALA: Sister-in-Law, the news has reached the city and the populace's gone insane. They are plundering the markets. We never dreamt our own people would go haywire like this. Suddenly, it's looters and marauders on the rampage everywhere. They're even attacking the temples. Even the sacred treasures of Vijaya Vittala are being pillaged.

SATYABHAMA: Is the palace safe?

TIRUMALA: That's it, Sister-in-Law. We have to vacate the palace. The ladies' quarters have to be emptied—immediately.

SATYABHAMA: Emptied?

TIRUMALA: Immediately. You, Amma, and all the queens and children have to leave. For Penukonda. I shall arrange for palanquins and carts.

SATYABHAMA (*calmly*): I'm not moving anywhere. Amma is in no condition to move out. She'll insist on waiting for her son. She lives for her son. The two of us will stay here. Let the Turukas raze the palace down. I'll wait for the Master and his brother. They'll come.

TIRUMALA: How can I tell you? The soldiers started fleeing headlong—when they saw Brother's head impaled on a spike.

(*Satyabhama screams and recoils in horror.*)

SATYABHAMA: Oh God! Oh mother! Are you sure? No, no, no! It can't be.

TIRUMALA: They all started deserting when they saw his—oh, horror! Severed head—the enemy beheaded him and exhibited his head. Took it around for all to see. That's when the flight began.

SATYABHAMA: I'd warned him. Not once, a hundred times! I told him we're growing old. He wouldn't listen. (*To the wailing women*) I said stop it. Instantly. Or I'll pull out your tongues. We are Kshatriyas—this is written in our foreheads. For sixty years I've lived in fear of this moment. Stop keening. Rajamma, lock up those hysterical women. Keep them locked up till I tell you. We have to look after Amma. We must see that we don't add to the disaster. Vengalamma, Chintamani, if you can't face your fate, go in and kill yourselves. Brother-in-Law, I'm not moving.

TIRUMALA: Try to understand. At the moment it's only the local goons. Our local thugs. Soon the marauders from surrounding regions will pour in and they'll be followed within the next couple of days by the Turukas—soldiers ravenous for plunder—and they won't care about the palace or the ladies' quarters. They are hungry, salivating beasts. There's no one here to fight them. It's going to be a free for all. Hell, sheer hell. When I said, empty the palace, I meant it. Every human being. Every bit of gold, jewellery, precious stones—

SATYABHAMA: That is your problem, Brother-in-Law. Ours is different. You haven't brought his body with you, have you, so we could plan our next step?

TIRUMALA: We—

SATYABHAMA: Don't. I'm not moving out of the palace. This is my home. I shall consume the special jaggery. It's been waiting on the shelf to be called into service all these years.

TIRUMALA: Please, please don't say that.

SATYABHAMA (*coldly*): No need for any melodrama. We're beyond that. I know and you know that you deserted the front. You betrayed my husband. You coward. You treacherous eunuch. Get out of my sight now.

TIRUMALA (*anguished*): Oh, Sister-in-Law!

SATYABHAMA: I asked you to stop him. I begged. And you did nothing. Well, it's all done now. I'm donating my possessions to the Gods. Please go in with Vengalamma and convey your orders to the women. Those who want to go to Penukonda can go. What you say is right. They would be wise to flee; this place is going to be worse than hell.

(*She goes in. Tirumala goes in with the maids.*)

Chambers of Sadashiva Raya

Sadashiva Raya, the puppet emperor of Vijayanagara, is about forty years old. He is being dressed, and like a bad tempered child is snarling at the attendant, Narasimha.

SADASHIVA: I'm certainly not moving out. Who's there to order me about now? You say Ramaraya is dead. Beheaded. Good for him. Should have happened long ago. Now I'm the ruler here. I am the King Emperor and no one can order me about.

NARASIMHA: People are rioting in the streets, sir. Things are getting worse every minute. Please hurry.

SADASHIVA: Watch your words. Remember you're talking to His Imperial Majesty. I am—

NARASIMHA (*suddenly harsh*): Listen, the Turukas are at the gate. If they find out who you are, you won't be left alive for five minutes.

SADASHIVA: If Vijayanagara's burning whose bloody fault is it? I was shouting out all the time. I sent word a hundred times, secure the city. Secure the city. Build walls round the city. Mount cannons. Nobody listened. Now I am taking charge—

(*Tirumala Raya rushes in.*)

TIRUMALA: Haven't you got him ready?

SADASHIVA: I'm not going anywhere, cousin.

TIRUMALA: Listen, you bloody idiot. You're alive because the courtiers want your high-class bottom on the throne. We could leave you here for those who may have a happier use for your arse, but we need that prestigious bum in Penukonda. Come on. Get moving.

SADASHIVA: How dare you. You're a coward, you treacherous bastard. You've fled from the battle abandoning your brother, your master. If you don't look out—

GUARD (*rushes in*): Sir, tragedy. The Queen Mother lay down on her bed and died.

(*Tirumala Raya gasps. But this is nothing unexpected.*)

SADASHIVA: Oh horror! Grand-aunt!

TIRUMALA (*bitterly*): She only lived for Ramaraya. She has nothing to live for now. (*To Narasimha*) Attend to this buffoon. But take care—keep him undamaged. He's precious.

(*Rushes out.*)

NARASIMHA (*shouts*): Pedda Nayaka! (*To Pedda Nayaka*) This Imperial Majesty has to be moved to Penukonda. If he makes too much trouble, tie him up. Gag him. Stuff him into a sack. But be careful. He's our guarantee of the throne—the most precious bauble we've got here in the palace. If anything happens to him, you and your whole platoon will pay with your necks.

(*A guard, more respectful, pushes Sadashiva out, protesting. Another one rushes in.*)

GUARD: Sir, more bad news. Queen Satyabhama too is dead. She lay down by the side of the Queen Mother and swallowed the special jaggery.

NARASIMHA: Good riddance. The fewer of these old hags we've to accommodate, the better. That'll mean more vehicles for the treasury, more carts to spare. Have all the mahouts been rounded up?

GUARD: Whoever is available. Not many left here.

NARASIMHA: No matter. Not a trinket from the palace is to be left behind. Load every one of the elephants. Also, the oxcarts and horses. Don't worry about the residents of the palace or the members of the royal family. They'll fend for themselves.

(*Pandemonium fills the sky.*)

ACT ONE

SCENE THREE

Vijayanagara, 1559

Vijayanagara at the height of its glory. The main square in the city, milling with crowds. The Vijayanagara heralds sound the drums and announce:

HERALDS:

Jaya jaya swasti samasta sadgunastoma bhadra

Kalyana Mahipala bhaskara

Vijayanagara Simhasanadheeshvara

Hinduraya Suratrana

Shree Ramaraja

Bho Paraak! Bho Paraak!

(*Ramaraya, ruler of Vijayanagara, enters. He is in his mid-seventies. Accompanying him are his two brothers, Venkatadri—about seventy—and Tirumala Raya—about sixty-five, followed by an enormous entourage.*

Ali Adil Shah, Sultan of Bijapur, enters from the other side. He is eighteen, energetic, and has a charming demeanour. He has very few people in his entourage, but they are all dressed in all their finery. The heralds thump their heavy staffs and announce:)

HERALDS:

Adab-Nigaah Ruu-BaRuu

Jahan Panah Qalandar Shabaah

Abu'al- Muzaffar Sultan Ali Adil Shah

Padshah-e-Bijapur!

(*They thump their staffs again. Ramaraya and Ali Adil Shah embrace.*)

RAMARAYA: Welcome, Sultan Ali Adil Shah, Lord and Master of Bijapura. You have brought honour and glory to the city of Vijayanagara by visiting it.

ADIL SHAH: May the hand of God protect Suratrana Ramaraya, Master of Vijayanagar, from all evil and lead him to greater glory.

RAMARAYA: This is an unprecedented honour. My city awaits your arrival with immense eagerness, led by my family.

ADIL SHAH: Sir, I am a prince of Bijapur, but I have grown up in the immense shadow of Ramaraya, the Lord of Vijayanagar, who towers over the whole of the Deccan. To meet you now, in person, is a privilege I never thought was written in my horoscope. But for that meeting to happen in the city of Vijayanagar places me among the chosen of the Heavens.

RAMARAYA: Come, honoured Sultan, meet my two brothers: the elder one is Venkatadri, the younger Tirumala Raya. They are here to take your commands.

ADIL SHAH: Who hasn't heard of them? They're not just your brothers, they're your two arms, the pillars of your glorious empire. We in the Deccan know of their immense military prowess, not merely by their reputation, but by having on occasion even experienced it personally.

(*Laughter. They are amazed by his ability to laugh at himself.*)

Sir, we heard of the tragedy that has befallen your family and are greatly stricken. Suratrana Ramaraya's loss is our loss too, your pain is ours. Our heart bleeds for your family. We had to rush to Vijayanagar to be by your side in this moment of grief.

RAMARAYA: It's God's will. Why Destiny should have called away our youngest son, the one nearest to our heart, is beyond our comprehension. We are surely paying for some misdemeanor in our past life, which is beyond human questioning and we bow before it.

ADIL SHAH: I am young and do not possess the authority to advise a person of your experience and eminence. Any attempt on my part to offer consolation would be only to make an exhibition of my infant intellect. But my Sufi guru has sent words for you: Death is only a merging of the human soul with the Divine. There *prakriti* and *purusha* come together, become one. It is to be taken as divine invitation to the human soul for union with the Ultimate.

RAMARAYA: Shahzada, the moment you heard of our loss, you've come rushing down from Bijapura to our city to share our grief, with a tiny company of five hundred horsemen, heedless of the discomfort and danger to your royal person. It is an unprecedented gesture, unmatched not merely for the courage but for the affection and trust you have displayed. We are struck speechless by your humanity.

ADIL SHAH: Suratrana, actually it's our turn to stand speechless: how can we even absorb this hospitality which is so warm and human despite its super-human grandeur? From the moment we crossed the River Krishna and stepped on its southern shore, we've been greeted at every step by a generosity and love beyond our wildest dreams.

RAMARAYA: The River Krishna shall bind us henceforth, Sultan, not divide us. It shall be the belt that binds our realms together.

ADIL SHAH: We'd heard so much about the beauty and wealth of the city of Vijayanagar. But having entered it we are unable to believe our own eyes. Its grandeur literally scares us. The wide avenues, the gardens, the landscaped terraces. And then the open markets selling precious stones and silks and rare scents—goods brought in here from distant corners of the world. It's what we read about in *Alif Laila*, but thought was fantasy.

RAMARAYA: Those are the blessings garnered from the deeds of our ancestors.

ADIL SHAH: A few moments ago my general, Kishwar Khan, was whispering to me that jewellery and gold and silver seem to sell here by the roadside like we sell vegetables and meat in Bijapur. The whole city, he gasped, looks like an open treasure house.

(*In the meantime, robes are brought in and exchanged.*)

RAMARAYA: It's your people that have opened for us the gates to the world outside and it's thanks to the bridges you have built that this wealth pours into our coffers. It's your gift to us. But the emotional richness you're offering to us is worth a million such gifts.

ADIL SHAH: I have a humble request. If this is far above our station, we must ask you to forgive our audacity.

RAMARAYA: The Sultan need hide no feeling of his from us.

ADIL SHAH: Please forget the sorrow you feel on losing your son. I am young and have had no father in my life. I am aware I am nowhere near worthy, but I beg the Suratrana to let me fill the emptiness left by your son's absence. May I have the privilege of calling myself your son?

(*Exclamations of wonder and appreciation from the people around.*)

RAMARAYA (*overcome*): What words! What love sculpted in angelic language! Let me speak the truth. I did not expect such a response from you, Sultan. Who would have dared to even imagine it? What am I to say in reply?

ADIL SHAH: Your majesty has to say nothing except yes. Accept me as your offspring, please.

(*Overwhelmed by emotion, Ramaraya draws Adil Shah into his arms.*)

'Appa-ji'! I now know I can call you Appa-ji, may your palm be on my head forever blessing me. Henceforth no honorifics for me, I beg you. Call me, *farzand*. I am privileged if you admit me into that little corner of your family.

RAMARAYA: A man has no right to adopt a son alone. It has to be done in conjunction; by the couple together. Come with me. Queen Satyabhama's waiting to welcome you in the chandrashala.

ADIL SHAH: The ladies' quarters! I'm lost for words.

(*They enter the chandrashala. Satyabhama is waiting there with the other queens and residents of the ladies' quarters.*)

SATYABHAMA: Welcome. Welcome to the Scion of Bijapura.

(*She and then a couple of other women raise the arati to his face. Put* kumkum *on his forehead. Adil Shah touches her feet.*)

ADIL SHAH: I bow to you, Amma-ji. Please accept me as your own child. If I can wipe away even a couple of the tears you've shed for your son, I shall be blessed.

(*Satyabhama and Ramaraya raise him up by his shoulders, 'smell the crown of his head' in the traditional fashion.*)

Henceforth, Ramaraya, the Lord of Vijayanagar, is my Appa-ji. Queen Satyabhama is my Amma-ji.

SATYABHAMA (*smiles*): No, no, Amma is enough.

(*Laughter all round.*)

RAMARAYA (*to the courtiers surrounding them*): Hear ye! From this moment, Sultan Ali Adil Shah is our farzand.

(*Exclamations of joy, happiness, approval.*)

SATYABHAMA: Why have you come alone, farzand? You should have brought your family with you to Hampi.

ADIL SHAH: I have no wife (*pause*)—not yet (*laughter*). Besides, we were concerned that those accompanying me may not want to return to Bijapur after tasting the delectation of Vijayanagar.

SATYABHAMA: And why should they return? The longer their stay, the happier we shall be.

ADIL SHAH: We didn't have the slightest doubt on that score.

RAMARAYA: Come, farzand. Mother is keen to meet you.

ADIL SHAH (*taken aback*): Your mother! This is beyond our wildest expectation.

(*They move to where Tirumalamba, Ramaraya's mother, is waiting. She is ninety-two, almost blind and nearly deaf.*)

RAMARAYA: Amma, the Sultan of Bijapura is here to pay respects to you.

ADIL SHAH (*loudly*): I have come seeking your *ashirvaads*—

(*For the first time since stepping into Vijayanagara, he is lost for the correct term, since he had not anticipated being introduced to Ramaraya's mother. He plunges on.*)

—Dadimaa.

(*Those around smile, sympathetically. He prostrates himself in front of her. She raises him and caresses his face fondly.*)

TIRUMALAMBA: From Bijapura? It's like the other end of the world. May God give you good fortune. Live and rule in glory. You remind me of our darling Chinna Tamma. A golden boy. We don't know what we did to anger the Gods, that we lost him.

ADIL SHAH: Dadima, I lost my mother's embrace in my childhood. I plead with you to take me up in your arms.

TIRUMALAMBA: May you live forever, son. Ramaraya, he is a royal guest. You will introduce him to Sadashiva, won't you? He will be very happy.

RAMARAYA: Have no worry, Amma. I was just leading him to the imperial quarters.

(*They move to Ramaraya's chambers. Ramaraya speaks in a low voice.*)

You realize, farzand, what Amma suggests is correct. His Imperial Majesty Sadashiva Raya, Emperor of Vijayanagara, should have been here to welcome you in person.

ADIL SHAH: We are also eager to pay our respects to His Imperial Majesty.

RAMARAYA: He too was most keen. But what could we do? The Court Astrologer has declared that the stars are not propitious for such a meeting, and that His Imperial Majesty should not step out of his chambers during this fortnight. We are helpless.

ADIL SHAH: We shall come again to attend his court.

RAMARAYA: Well, you must be exhausted after your long day. Shall we move to your chambers? Your entourage must be waiting for you.

(*Adil Shah nods. However, they have not discussed the main issue, and he is unable to hide the disappointment on his face. Ramaraya notices it and signals to their companions. All except Tirumala and Venkatadri retire from the scene.*)

RAMARAYA: Farzand, do you know what has touched me deeply today? You've come from Bijapura with only a posse of five hundred riders, braving all the perils of the road. That's amazing enough. But more than that, you have walked into our palace alone, without any bodyguards. The palace is surrounded by our men and there's no one anywhere nearby from your side. Not a soul. You could come to any harm.

ADIL SHAH (*smiles*): The thought never occurred to me.

RAMARAYA: That's your greatness. But what about your bodyguards? They're stationed half a *kos* away from the palace and know that you are nowhere within their reach. My messengers inform me that they stand there trembling and sweating in dread—praying for your safety—and no doubt, for their own. And who would blame them? I doubt if I would've put my son in such a calamitous position. And I'm at a loss to know how to respond to your—courage? Daredevilry? Rashness? How can I show my appreciation of this trust—which strikes me as nothing short of foolhardy?

ADIL SHAH: As you know, my father made attempts on my life in our own palace. I couldn't be in a safer place than here, Appa-ji.

RAMARAYA (*suddenly*): You want the fort of Kalyana, don't you?

(*Adil Shah is taken aback. For once, he is lost for words.*)

Don't you?

ADIL SHAH (*trying to recover*): Is there anything you don't know under the skies of Deccan?

RAMARAYA: You've written to Sultan Hussain Nizam Shah of Ahmadnagar asking him to surrender the forts of Kalyana and Raichur to you. Haven't you?

ADIL SHAH (*fumbling*): As you're well aware—

RAMARAYA: And you're quite right. As the Sultan of Bijapura you have every right over Kalyana. It was in the possession of Bijapura until I intervened and handed it over to Nizam Shah ten years ago.

ADIL SHAH: And you were fully justified, sir, in that transfer. My father's insanity drove him to actions which were unpardonable. He insulted your ambassadors, abused your authority.

RAMARAYA: And for the last ten years Kalyana has been in the Nizam's possession. Long enough, don't you think?

ADIL SHAH: Appa-ji, it would be arrogant on my part to even try and express a comment on what was your considered decision.

RAMARAYA: Well, your father's dead now. May his soul rest in peace! And I hereby entrust Kalyana back to your family.

(*Venkatadri and Tirumala are stunned by Ramaraya's remark. They look at each other flabbergasted. Adil Shah listens unable to say anything while Ramaraya continues, almost talking to himself.*)

Kalyana! Kalyana! The source of my lineage—the fountain from which my forefathers sprang—the city of the great Chalukyas! That's where the seed of my family took root, sprouted, branched out, blossomed, reached out for the heavens—But as fortune has ordained, today I bear the responsibility of looking after the empire of Vijayanagara. All I can do is look at my ancestral city of Kalyana from a distance, across the River Krishna, while my own arms are loaded with responsibilities my father-in-law, Krishna Raya, has nailed me down with. Can you imagine anything more heart-rending? But I cannot abandon Kalyana to aliens. I have to ensure its welfare. When Barid Shah started misbehaving, I took it away and gave it to Nizam Shah. But now that the bonds of Vijayanagara and Bijapura have been soldered together again I shall entrust it to you. Kalyana! My Kalyana! Please, please, farzand, look after it with care.

(*He is emotionally overcome and wipes his tears. Adil Shah suddenly kneels in front of him in gratitude. Ramaraya gently raises him up.*)

ADIL SHAH: You have my word, Appa-ji.

RAMARAYA (*wiping his tears*): Are you happy, son? Time to retire, isn't it?

ADIL SHAH: May I make a final request? Your reputation as a player of the *veena* equals the fame of your expertise with the sceptre. Would you please consider playing a *dhun* for me some time?

RAMARAYA: I'm happiest when I'm with my veena. I see I have entrusted Kalyana to the right person. Come. Why later? Right now. Let's proceed to the music room.

Venkatadri, send word to Sultan Hussain Nizam Shah that we should like the guardianship of the fort of Kalyana to be transferred to the care of Bijapura. Tell him we shall brook no dilly-dallying on the issue. When our farzand leaves, accompany him with a battalion of one lakh cavalry to Kalyana and ensure that Nizam Shah behaves himself when he receives our request.

(*Ramaraya exits with Ali Adil Shah. Venkatadri and Tirumala stand digesting these new developments.*)

TIRUMALA: Brother Venkatadri, what do you think?

VENKATADRI: What's there to think? He won't listen to us. (*Pause.*) I don't know why we're provoking Nizam Shah.

TIRUMALA: Actually, that I don't mind. I'm rearing for a fight and should be happy to go with Adil Shah. Can you please—suggest it to him?

VENKATADRI: You think Brother will listen?

TIRUMALA (*explodes*): Why is he treating me like this? Why is he pushing me away from the field of action into a dead corner? Will he never forgive me my one little lapse?

(*Venkatadri shrugs. The strains of veena are heard in the background. They move in.*)

SCENE FOUR

Inner Chamber in the Palace at Ahmadnagar

Sultan Hussain Nizam Shah is being nursed and bandaged by Hakim Qasim Beg, while his queen, Begum Humayun Sultana, is in attendance.

HAKIM: It is imperative that the Sultan stay at home and rest for at least another two months. We've had this ointment sent down from the city of Qum, made by an apothecary there whose family has developed it and kept its ingredients secret. Let the body derive its full benefits before the Sultan sets out on anything strenuous.

NIZAM SHAH: I understand.

BEGUM (*flaring up*): The Sultan understands nothing. Please, at least be honest with the honourable Hakim. And don't tell lies. It's a question of your health. (*To the Hakim*) You see how blandly he promises to stay at home and rest. He won't. He can't stay in bed for an hour. He will say, 'I understand', to you, but has just ordered our troops to be ready to march.

HAKIM: It's a wondrous medicine. But how can it be effective if we don't let it run its own course?

BEGUM (*to the Hakim*): Do you think he's even listening to you? An Ottoman gun founder is making a bronze muzzle-loader for him on the bastion of our fort. That's all he is thinking about.

HAKIM: I need not point out that the Master's health is more important than the state of the muzzle-loader, which can be repaired and improved at will. But the whole responsibility of looking after Ahmadnagar rests on the shoulders of the Sultan. While I urge him to take rest, let me not say I am unaware of the gravity of his task. (*Getting up*) I've finished for the day. I shall need to have a look again tomorrow. In the meantime, if the limbs hurt, apply poultice. I take leave of you.

BEGUM: The carriage will come for you as usual tomorrow morning.

HAKIM: God be with you.

(*The Hakim bows and retires.*)

BEGUM: Are you hurting badly?

(*She starts applying poultice to his limbs.*)

NIZAM SHAH (*whispers to himself*): No news from Barid. That's worrying.

BEGUM: What's it? What're you mumbling?

NIZAM SHAH (*abashed*): Nothing. Nothing.

BEGUM: You've started talking to yourself these days. Something about—

NIZAM SHAH (*brusquely*): I said, 'Nothing.'

(*Pause.*)

BEGUM: The news from Vijayanagar hasn't even been confirmed. And you're itching to leave!

NIZAM SHAH: What do you expect me to do? Adil Shah's left for Kalyan accompanied by a detachment under Venkatadri. That's confirmed. I know what Ramaraya's demand will be and I must be prepared.

(*Pause.*)

I'm not surprised by Ramaraya. It's Adil Shah who astounds me! In front of the whole populace of Vijayanagar, he apparently fell at Ramaraya's feet and called him his father. It beggars belief!

BEGUM: Adil Shah was locked up by his father for years, and none of you moved a finger to help him. Now, he wants someone to help him, someone who *can* help him. What did you expect him to do? After all, it was Ramaraya who gifted the fort of Kalyan to us. So let's not be sanctimonious. Now, Adil Shah wants his turn. He's doing exactly what you did ten years ago.

(*Nizam Shah has no answer.*)

Have you thought of how long you all are going to go on like this—accepting alms from Ramaraya? Today, he wants Kalyan to be handed over to Bijapur. Tomorrow, he'll say give it to Golkonda. Then, he'll say it's the turn of Bidar. And you'll wait around him—bowing and scraping—salivating?

NIZAM SHAH: Watch your tongue! This time I've said it. 'No. I'll not yield.' I've told Adil Shah he will not get the fort. I've made that clear to Ramaraya as well.

BEGUM: And will he listen? Do any of you have the strength to say no to that brute?

NIZAM SHAH: You know perfectly well the answer to that. Ramaraya straddles the whole of the Deccan. And he has two brothers, brilliant generals. They only have to flick their fingers and a whole swarm of support armies will pour in from every corner of the empire.

BEGUM: So you'll yield to every whim of his?

NIZAM SHAH: What do you want me to do? Ramaraya will not negotiate. He insists that the fort go to Adil Shah. (*Pause.*) It's maddening! The fort of Kalyan is outside the borders of his realm. It's inside my borders. Why in the name of Heaven is he meddling in my politics?

(*Pause.*)

BEGUM: Actually, I feel sorry for his wife.

NIZAM SHAH: Whose wife? Ramaraya's? What's she got to do with it?

BEGUM: Her father built the empire of Vijayanagar. Her husband should have succeeded him to the throne. But the royal family and the courtiers won't let him come near the throne because he is of a lower caste. So there's dear Ramaraya! Married to the princess of Vijayanagar and denied the throne! The royal son-in-law! And yet he is the all-powerful ruler; they can't do without him. So instead of being the imperial consort, she is the low-class Son-in-Law's wife. In her own father's imperial palace! Can you imagine anything more humiliating? It's bound to gnaw at her innards—and when something gnaws at the wife's innards, it sucks out the husband's blood too.

(*Nizam Shah smiles wrily.*)

So he's trying to claim a royal lineage for himself—the Chalukyas of Kalyan.

NIZAM SHAH: A bogus claim. Pure fantasy.

BEGUM: Everyone needs a fantasy to live by. The Sultans. The people. Everyone.

NIZAM SHAH: The Chalukya dynasty disappeared from this earth four hundred years ago. There isn't even a Chalukya puppy left in the streets of Kalyan.

(*Pause.*)

BEGUM: Our maid Khatija has in-laws working in the stables of Vijayanagar. That's a whirlpool that sucks in gossip from the world over. She says the city hates Ramaraya. They want to throw him out. The royal family is fulminating at how he is treating the heir to the throne—like a chained dog. You could sound them out—

NIZAM SHAH: To do what? Rise against Ramaraya? Those idiot vassals have headaches of their own and all they want is a stable power at the centre. Why don't you women keep to what you understand? It's not for nothing that they say that a woman's brains are below her knees.

BEGUM (*calmly*): So what're you going to do? Submit to his demands?

NIZAM SHAH (*exasperated*): What do you want me to do?

BEGUM: Talk to the other Sultans. Make them see the danger. I know you all despise each other. But Barid Shah, Qutb Shah—surely they're not so stupid that they cannot see that this calamity will hit them too one day.

NIZAM SHAH: Forty thousand horses are sold in the market of Bidar. You know who buys most of them? Vijayanagar. They keep Barid Shah's coffers full. When Qutb Shah's brother tried to assassinate him, you know where he fled? To Vijayanagar. He hung around in that city for ten years. Ramaraya knows they're all beholden to him. He knows he can twist them round his fingers.

BEGUM: I hear that only the other day some of Ramaraya's forces passing through the outskirts of Bidar looted markets and desecrated masjids.

NIZAM SHAH (*taken aback*): The news has already reached you? I wish I could recruit some of your maids in my secret service.

BEGUM: Surely that desecration was not accidental. Ramaraya must've known what his ruffians were up to.

(*Pause.*)

NIZAM SHAH: Begum, at this moment the forces of Vijayanagar are marching on Kalyan along with Adil Shah's troops. That's a fact I've got to face. I've got to do something about it. I have only two choices. Hand over the fort to Adil Shah and expose myself as a craven fool in the eyes of the other Sultans. Or fight and make a fool of myself.

(*Pause.*)

BEGUM: May I suggest something? If you promise not to lose your temper.

NIZAM SHAH (*weary*): Go ahead. What is it?

BEGUM: God has blessed us with four daughters. Chand Bibi is already the toast of the town. For her looks. Her brains. She is so bright she scares me. Then Bibi Jamaal? Not bright. A bit on the darker side. But she's got her eyes and nose in the right place.

NIZAM SHAH: And so?

BEGUM: Why don't we offer Chand Bibi to Adil Shah in marriage? We've had requests for her from Isphahan and Tashkent. Adil Shah will not decline. He wants the fort of Kalyan, doesn't he? Gift it to Chand Bibi as our present to her.

(*Nizam Shah is aghast at the suggestion.*)

Qutb Shah will accept Bibi Jamaal—if she comes with the forts of Mudgal or Sholapur.

NIZAM SHAH: Bravo! Bravo! How brilliant! Haven't you got an iota of sense left? Adil Shah apparently spends all his time chanting and swaying in the company of Sufi mendicants. I doubt if he'll last even a few months on the throne. Qutb is a wimp, immersed in music and Telugu poetry. Why don't we just kill our daughters instead?

BEGUM: Our daughters will live as they are fated. Let's worry about our fate.

NIZAM SHAH: No. I refuse. Look, leave this to the men and you look after the affairs of the *zenana*.

(*Begum moves away. Pause. Nizam Shah starts talking to himself in a low voice.*)

NIZAM SHAH: If only Barid would reply. Jahangir Khan. That's the man.

BEGUM: There you go. Burbling to yourself again.

NIZAM SHAH (*abashed*): What did I say?

BEGUM: Something about Jahangir Khan.

NIZAM SHAH (*avoiding her question*): I am the Sultan of Ahmadnagar and if I have to fight alone for my pride, I shall do so. If I'm defeated, so be it.

BEGUM: God will grant us victory. Rest now.

(*She covers him with a blanket and moves off. He shuts his eyes. She starts praying.*)

SCENE FIVE

Vijayanagara, 1561

The square in front of the palace. Scattered crowds. Sadashiva Raya in full imperial regalia, flanked by Ramaraya, Tirumala Raya, Satyabhama, and others, all dressed up for the occasion.

HERALDS:

Shreeman Maharajadhiraja Parameshwara

Veerapratapa Shriveera Pampapureshwara

Tuluva Vamsha Bhaskara

Sadashivadeva Maharaja

Vijayeebhava Vijayeebhava

Victory to His Imperial Majesty Sadashivaraja, Lord of Vijayanagara, Scion of the Tuluva dynasty, Blessed of Lord Pampapati.

(*The crowds disperse. Tirumala signals to Sadashiva to move back into the palace.*)

SADASHIVA: Not much of a crowd this year.

(*Tirumala shakes his head dourly.*)

And it gets thinner every year.

(*No response.*)

Not too many of your relations turned up. They don't think they need to pay their respects to the Emperor?

TIRUMALA: They knew the *muhurta*. They turn up every year. Don't know why such a poor turnout today. (*Pause*) We sent word. It's their duty to attend. But one can't arm-twist them into attending.

SADASHIVA: You would have if you had decided to. Perhaps the Aravidu family has decided they don't need to pay tribute to their Emperor.

TIRUMALA (*shrugs*): We'll find out.

SADASHIVA (*contemptuously*): Find out. Yes, do. (*As Tirumala guides him towards the palace*) What about Grand Aunt's blessings?

TIRUMALA: She's not feeling well.

SADASHIVA: Nonsense. She's perfectly all right. That's the first thing I checked this morning. I was expecting this. (*Firmly*) I have to see Grand Aunt. These are my commands.

(*Sadashiva's raised voice and angry demeanour are beginning to attract the attention of the thinning crowd. They begin to stop and listen.*)

I'm not asking for permission to see an enemy of the State, you know. I only want to pay respects to Grand Aunt—mother to the whole palace. Among the Aravidu clan, she's the only one to have always treated me as her own. Embraced me as one of hers. Don't I even have the right to take her blessings?

(*Slowly losing temper*)

I know the Turuka Adil Shah was admitted to her presence. He was taken into the ladies' quarters. Then why am I, the Emperor, being denied permission?

(*No reaction from anyone.*)

I shall not enter the palace without seeing her. Cousin Satyabhama ... Please.

(*Tears well up in Satyabhama's eyes. Ramaraya looks at Satyabhama and relents.*)

RAMARAYA: All right. Let him meet Amma. Venkatadri has sent messengers from Kalyana. I'll see them first and join you.

(*Ramaraya departs with his attendants.*)

SADASHIVA (*to Satyabhama*): This is how they treat the royal family. You're a Tuluva, Cousin Satyabhama. Doesn't it upset you to see our Tuluva bloodline treated like this?

(*The question obviously stings. Satyabhama stifles her distress and with the others enters the chandrashala where Tirumalamba is resting. Tirumala Raya follows with Sadashiva.*)

SADASHIVA: I fall at your feet, Grand Aunt.

TIRUMALAMBA: Who, Sadashiva? Come, son. I'm so happy to see you. My eyes are gone but I am happy you remember this old woman. Come, come, sit here by me. How was the *darshan* this morning?

(*Sadashiva does not respond. Tirumalamba turns to Satyabhama who turns away.*)

TIRUMALA: There was a huge attendance, Amma. There always is. The people of Hampi yearn for the Emperor's darshan. They would go out of control if we didn't keep a strict watch on them.

TIRUMALAMBA: A darshan once a year is not enough. We should arrange it more often. Tell Ramaraya.

TIRUMALA: And this year there were hordes of foreigners. From China, from Egypt.

TIRUMALAMBA: I so wanted to attend the ceremony. See you on your throne. It's been so many years since I saw you in your glory. But what can one say to Old Age? My eyes have turned to pebbles. Knees are locked up. I ache all over. Why God keeps one alive so long I don't know. So how are you, son? Are you well?

(*No reply from Sadashiva.*)

What is it, Sadashiva? Is something bothering you? What could worry you? You are the Emperor of Vijayanagara.

SADASHIVA (*suddenly overcome with tears*): What can I say, Grand Aunt? Yes, I am the Emperor of Vijayanagara. Yes, I am the Supreme Ruler. But I would not wish my plight on a dog. I am tired. Crushed. I want to jump into the Tunga River and die.

TIRUMALAMBA: Please! You should not utter such dreadful things. What can the Emperor lack? The world's at your feet. Ask.

SADASHIVA: This is not a palace for me, Amma. It's a parrot's cage. A prison cell. For twenty years I have been in here—incarcerated—without permission to even peep out, let alone walk outside. You know I am not allowed into the streets. To talk to anyone. Not even to a beggar. I can't take five steps without being forced back.

(*Weeps. Tirumala tries to control him by holding him by his shoulder.*)

I don't have anyone to chat with. A simple chat.

TIRUMALAMBA: But who can stop you? You wear the imperial crown on your head. Who can deny you anything? What's this, Satyabhama?

(*Satyabhama turns away, hiding her feelings.*)

Tirumala? I don't understand. My brains have collapsed. Aren't you taking care of him?

TIRUMALA: Mother, you have nothing to worry about. We're there. Sadashivaraja is a sensitive soul. He hurts easily. But he is the King Emperor. The times are treacherous and we need to be vigilant at every step.

TIRUMALAMBA: The times are bad, Sadashiva. You must take care. It was not like this in the days of Krishna Raya. He roamed around the world with the army and yet we slept without any worries then.

SADASHIVA: I have so much I want to say. But who can I talk to? I don't want to bother you. But …

TIRUMALAMBA: Tell me, son. I need to know. I shall tell Ramaraya.

SADASHIVA: Grand Aunt, why was I not allowed to see the Sultan of Bijapura? That was my right as the King Emperor, wasn't it? There are other things I hear about, I want to talk about. Things that worry me as the Emperor. Look now. A whole contingent of cavalries is away fighting in Kalyana. And no one here to protect the city. Who's here to look after our security? We've two Afghan generals in our army. Brothers. And they were telling me that in the west when an army goes out to battle, they first ensure the protection of the capital. Care is taken to see that the capital is not vulnerable to surprise attacks. (*He gets excited as he waxes eloquent.*) We're wide open. We don't even have cannons mounted on the bastions or on the curtain walls. What we should have are semi-circular bastions, high and thick merlons, wide walkaways on the ramparts. Our moats are not deep or wide enough. You should hear the Afghans describe the innovations of cavaliers and barbicans. We only have stone walls erected without mortar which will crumble—

TIRUMALA: I must say that's most impressive. The Afghans seem to have nothing to do except give lessons in defence and His Imperial Majesty is evidently been a keen student! But let me assure you, Sadashiva, Brother Ramaraya is perfectly aware of the new developments in warfare. He has won every battle in the last thirty years. We're protected by the grace of Lord Virupaksha and in two hundred years no one has dared touch the outskirts of our city. Amma, the city has nothing to fear. But we shall take care of our Emperor. (*In a whisper to Sadashiva*) Is this something to discuss with Amma? Fool!

(*Ramaraya enters with his entourage.*)

RAMARAYA: So has the Imperial Majesty finished his confabulations with Amma?

TIRUMALAMBA: Why don't you let him out of the palace grounds, Ramaraya? He can't spend all his time confined even if it is for his safety.

RAMARAYA: Amma, your word is our command. (*Loudly*) Tirumala, will you please arrange a tour of the city and its parks for the Majesty every full moon day?

TIRUMALA: I'll see to it, Brother.

TIRUMALAMBA: He was also mentioning some suggestions the Turuka generals were making. Forts. Cannons. For the defence of the city.

(*Ramaraya stiffens at this.*)

RAMARAYA: Oh, those Turukas. Yes, yes, they are obsessed with firearms. Gunpowder and noisy explosions. We'll attend to it. May we now have your permission, Amma? Your Majesty—

SADASHIVA: I want your blessings, Grand Aunt. I wish I could see you before next year.

(*He prostrates before her. She blesses him. He departs with some attendants.*)

RAMARAYA: Who let him talk to the foreigners?

TIRUMALA: Difficult to control him. He's capable of making a scene.

RAMARAYA: He's never ever to be allowed to come in the presence of Amma again. Ever. Understand?

TIRUMALA: Yes, Brother.

RAMARAYA: In fact, there'll be no more public appearances of His Majesty. No darshans. Keep him locked up in the palace, running around inside like a rat.

TIRUMALA: But if we don't allow the public to view him at least once a year, rumours'll fly about.

RAMARAYA: There'll always be rumours sniping at us, while we nurse this imbecile on the throne. Our royal Tuluva relations need to use up the poison in their fangs.

(*Suddenly he keels over and grabs his neck. An attendant supports and seats him.*)

Oh, God! This cursed new problem. My head suddenly starts spinning like a Chinese lantern. Maddening. Absolutely infuriating. Wait! Wait!

(*He sits down holding his head.*)

TIRUMALA: Take some rest. You've had a long day. I'm glad Venkatadri has sent good news. Apparently, Nizam Shah was stupid enough to try and fight our forces. He didn't stand a chance. Problems of any other kind?

RAMARAYA: Of course there were problems. Adil Shah thinks he won the battle and has demanded to be given the keys to the fort of Kalyana. Venkatadri refused, point blank.

TIRUMALA: Good for him. (*Smiles*) And what was Adil Shah's reaction to that?

RAMARAYA: He sulked. As expected. He'll learn. We have to drive it into the Turukas that they can strut about, but we retain control.

TIRUMALA: So, Venkatadri has the keys to the fort?

RAMARAYA: No, I told Venkatadri to leave the keys with Nizam Shah. I shall take the keys from him, and then I shall hand over the keys to Adil Shah.

TIRUMALA: But Brother, you aren't going all the way to Kalyana just to take possession of the keys, are you?

RAMARAYA: Not Kalyana. I am going to Ahmadnagar. I have asked Nizam Shah to come there and hand the keys over to me. It's not enough to snatch Kalyana away from him. We need to take him down a peg or two in the eyes of his populace.

(*Pause.*)

In the meantime, Adil Shah shall go back to Bijapura and wait. (*Smiles*) For his keys.

SCENE SIX

The Camp in front of the Fort of Ahmadnagar

Venkatadri leads Nizam Shah in. Hakim Kasim Beg follows and waits in attendance at a distance.

VENKATADRI: Will the Sultan please take a seat?

(*Nizam Shah who is expecting Ramaraya to be there looks around in surprise.*)

Brother is resting. He will be here any moment.

NIZAM SHAH: We heard that the Hinduraya Suratrana's health was worrying. We hope he's well.

VENKATADRI: Indeed he is. He has an iron constitution. But recently he has started getting a whirling sensation in his head. But the *Vaidya* assures us it should be no cause for worry.

NIZAM SHAH: Honoured Venkatadri, may I say something? We cannot understand why Sri Ramaraya puts himself under such strain at his age. He has able support in you, in your younger brother Tirumala. Surely the Suratrana did not need to come all the way for such insignificant chores.

VENKATADRI (*smiles wryly*): True enough. But you know Brother. He likes to do everything himself.

NIZAM SHAH: The world is only too eager to misconstrue such energy as mistrust.

(*Venkatadri does not react. He is used to these insinuations.*)

HERALD:

Kalyana Mahipala Bhaskara Ramaraja Bho Parak.

All hail the glorious sun that shines as the King of Kalyana.

(*Ramaraya arrives supported by an attendant, and sits on the only seat available in the tent. Nizam Shah is offered no seat to sit on. He swallows his frustration and waits in attendance with a smile.*)

RAMARAYA: Salaam Alekum Hazrat Hussain Nizam Shah.

NIZAM SHAH: Waalekum Salaam to the Gola Suratrana of Vijayanagar.

RAMARAYA: May God's blessings ensure the well-being of the Sultan of Ahmadnagar.

NIZAM SHAH: We are indeed blessed to have the friendship of Suratrana Ramaraya.

RAMARAYA: We should have been happy to offer hospitality to the Sultan in our capital itself as we have to his illustrious colleague from Bijapura. But circumstances were such that we had to be content with this meeting.

NIZAM SHAH: Who in Deccan has the courage to decline when commanded by the Suratrana to come?

RAMARAYA (*laughs*): Command? God help us. Not a command. A request, let me say. An invitation. The Lord God has been kind enough to grant us all that we have wished for. We are content. We ask for nothing more—than the hand of your friendship.

NIZAM SHAH: Have we ever declined it to Vijayanagar?

RAMARAYA: If what you say is true why these recurrent conflicts between Ahmadnagar and Vijayanagara. Venkatadri, please read out to the Sultan the details of the conflicts we've had between us.

NIZAM SHAH: Danda Nayaka Venkatadri does not need to trouble himself. Every one of those battles is vividly present in our memory.

(*Pause.*)

The Master of Vijayanagar knows that we did not want this conflict. The Sultan of Ahmadnagar has no complaints against the ruler of Vijayanagar. This was merely a matter of minor adjustment between Ahmadnagar and Bijapur. We fail to understand how Vijayanagar got drawn into it.

RAMARAYA: Sultan Ali Adil Shah has extended to us his hand of friendship—indeed, of kinship.

NIZAM SHAH: The whole of Deccan rejoices at this development. It will indeed be our great good fortune if the Suratrana displays the same benevolence to the other Sultans as well.

RAMARAYA (*suddenly decides to bring this mock formality to a close*): You are in possession of the fort of Kalyana. We would like it to be handed over to Sultan Ali Adil Shah. That's all.

NIZAM SHAH: The fort was in fact in the possession of Bijapur ten years ago and it was handed over to us by none other than you. We can say with pride that we have showered all our attention on its safety and security. We fail to understand why now—

RAMARAYA: We are not in the habit of explaining our decisions to anyone.

NIZAM SHAH: We are neighbours. If there's been a lapse on our part—

RAMARAYA: You've had Kalyana for ten years. Enough! Now let Bijapura have his turn.

NIZAM SHAH: We are helpless if the—

(*Ramaraya suddenly cuts him by moaning and lurching as though he is losing his balance. He grabs his forehead. An attendant rushes in and starts massaging his forehead. Venkatadri too steps forward but Ramaraya shoos him away. He snarls at the attendant.*)

RAMARAYA: Here. Here you fool. A little further back. Idiot. Yes. That's better.

(*suddenly friendly, still holding his forehead, to Nizam Shah*)

Surely I don't need to explain such an elementary point. There are four of you Sultans on my northern border. And I need to keep you under firm control. Vigilance is of the essence. Is that clear? Enough. Venkatadri, have you informed the honourable Sultan of our terms?

VENKATADRI: Yes, Brother. We have.

RAMARAYA: And they're acceptable to him?

NIZAM SHAH: Please, Suratrana. I only—

RAMARAYA (*with a show of exasperation*): Nothing's ever simple. Read the clauses of the agreement, Venkatadri. Only to refresh our memories and not for discussion.

VENKATADRI: First, Badshah Hussain Nizam Shah of Ahmadnagar shall hand over the keys to the fort of Kalyana to Sultan Adil Shah of Bijapura. We shall take the keys and convey them to the Sultan.

(*Nizam Shah, without a word, signals. A large plate is brought to him on which are placed the keys to the fort of Kalyana. Being symbolic, they are larger than life. Nizam Shah picks up the keys with an immense sense of responsibility and hands them over to Ramaraya.*)

NIZAM SHAH: The keys to the gate of Kalyan. I am handing them over to the Suratrana of Vijayanagar for conveyance to Sultan Adil Shah of Bijapur. We beg to be excused for any lapses on our part.

(*Ramaraya picks the keys up and reverently touches his forehead with them.*)

RAMARAYA: Kalyana! Kalyana! The source of the hallowed dynasty of the Chalukyas. The source from where my bloodline flows. (*Overcome*) My eternal *namaskaras* to the founders of Kalyana, my Chalukya forefathers.

Venkatadri, please dispatch this heirloom to Bijapura, guarded by ten thousand cavalry! My bequest to my farzand, Ali Adil Shah. Son, take good care of this treasure.

(*Emotionally overwhelmed, he sits on the chair, staring at the keys as they are taken away. Pause.*)

Next?

VENKATADRI (*unsure*): Jahangir Khan, commander of the fort of Ahmadnagar during all these days, to be beheaded.

NIZAM SHAH (*astounded*): But I thought—I thought—I had made a special plea—I thought this term had been softened to—please! I beg of you.

RAMARAYA: Yes, you have. But we have not changed our mind.

NIZAM SHAH: Have mercy, Raya Bhupati. Please do not insist—I clutch your feet.

RAMARAYA: I fail to understand completely. I'm only asking for the head of a minor army officer from Bidar. Not one of your men. Why are you so overwrought?

NIZAM SHAH: That's precisely it, sir. He is not in my service. I borrowed him from Barid Shah. You may ask for the head of anyone in my employ, and it'll be yours. I'm willing to surrender my own head.

RAMARAYA: Come on, Sultan. You wouldn't expect us to make such an absurd request. You are our guest. It's our *dharma* to see that you are not harmed. (*Laughs.*) Your head. Honestly! We have fought so many battles. Lost and won so many. Has it ever been suggested that the Chief of the Kingdom be harmed? *Shantam paapam*!

NIZAM SHAH (*anguished*): That speaks for the immense generosity of the Raya Bhupati, for the humanity of Vijayanagar. Your power has never endangered our lives personally. I seek the same generosity in the case of Jahangir Khan.

RAMARAYA (*explodes*): Who is this Jahangir Khan? What is he to us? Who brought him in here?

NIZAM SHAH: I did, sir. I confess. I take the blame for it. When I had to leave Ahmadnagar to face you in Kalyan, I needed someone to protect my capital. Someone I could entrust the lives of wives and children to. And Sultan Barid Shah sent him as one of his trusted men. Jahangir Khan was only following his master's orders. He's come to look after the safety of my people. What will the world say if I don't protect a man who came to protect my family? It'll be a stigma my family will never wash off.

RAMARAYA: He wouldn't surrender even after we informed him you had laid down arms in Kalyana.

NIZAM SHAH: I'd asked him to wait for my orders. He was only being faithful to his instructions. He waited until I'd confirmed the outcome.

(*Ramaraya has lost interest in Nizam Shah's words.*)

RAMARAYA: Where's this Jahangir Khan?

NIZAM SHAH: There, sir, there. He is positioned on the western rampart of the fort. There. So you can see him.

(*They come out of the tent to look at the fort. Jahangir Khan, hands tied and gagged, is standing on a bastion, with an executioner by his side.*)

NIZAM SHAH: My wife, my family, the entire populace of Ahmadnagar, is watching at this moment. They are praying for his life. Please, sir, I plead with you. The honour of my family is at stake (*starts weeping*).

RAMARAYA: I had never thought I'd ever meet a person who would reduce the dauntless Nizam Shah to tears. Venkatadri, is everything ready?

VENKATADRI (*crushed*): Yes, Brother.

RAMARAYA: Jahangir Khan's head will roll the moment I give the signal?

VENKATADRI: Yes, Brother.

(*Ramaraya raises his hand to signal. A gun goes off. Nizam Shah covers his eyes in horror. The executioner forces Jahangir Khan to a crouching position with his head on a block and the axe ready. Ramaraya gives the signal. The cannon goes off. The executioner beheads Jahangir Khan. Nizam Shah writhes as though in sudden severe pain.*)

RAMARAYA: What's this, sir? You've witnessed thousands of men being slaughtered. You've slaughtered them with your own hands. And so have I. This is not an issue to be given much cognizance. A small price surely for eternal peace and friendship between us.

Console yourself, Sultan. You have fulfilled both my conditions. There's no further need for any tension between us. We are friends now. Come, Vijayanagara stretches its hand of brotherhood to you.

(*He stretches both his hands towards Nizam Shah, who stands ignoring him. Ramaraya's tone gets harsher.*)

Badshah Hussain Nizam Shah, Vijayanagara is stretching its hand to Ahmadnagar.

(*Nizam Shah stands up, arms outstretched. Nizam Shah, as though in a daze, moves to him without any emotion and carefully takes the tips of Ramaraya's fingers in his hands. Ramaraya holds on to Nizam Shah's finger tips.*)

May this bond of ours last forever.

(*Turns to his attendant.*)

Paan.

(*The attendant brings a plate carrying paan. Nizam Shah stares at his own fingers in disgust as though they were dirty. He signals to his attendant to bring him a jar of water on a plate. Nizam Shah stretches his hands on the plate and looks at Hakim Qasim Beg who pours water on them. Nizam Shah washes his fingers with deliberate slowness, rubbing each finger carefully. Then, he takes a piece of cloth and dries his fingers ostentatiously, as Ramaraya glares from a distance.*)

RAMARAYA (*aside to Venkatadri*): If he wasn't here as my guest today, I would've chopped off his arms and strung them round his neck.

(*Then Ramaraya too orders a jug of water and washes his fingers. He dries his fingers, and picks up the paan and offers it to Nizam Shah.*

When Nizam Shah tries to take it by hand, Ramaraya shakes his head and indicates that Nizam Shah should let him place the paan in his mouth. The latter reluctantly accepts it.)

Vijayanagara is famed for its betel leaves. They have no match in the world for the red colour they bring to the lips. The Sultan should order some for his zenana.

(*Without waiting for Nizam Shah to start chewing the paan, Ramaraya covering his eyes with both his palms bows low in mock farewell and leaves. But Venkatadri and the others watch as Nizam Shah steps toward Ahmadnagar, stands with his back to the city and viciously spits out his mouthful on to the ground.*)

ACT TWO

SCENE SEVEN

The stage is divided into two halves. The left half represents a decorated hall in Bijapur, while the right half represents a section of the palace in Golconda. Nikkah *ceremonies are in progress parallelly in the two sections.*

In both places, elders—all male—are gathered in the front area where the nikkah will be performed. This area has chilmans *hung in the background behind which the ladies are gathered.*

In the Bijapur section, the bridegroom is Ali Adil Shah, flanked by the Qazi, Nizam Shah, and the elite among the invited.

On the Golconda side, the same arrangement prevails, except that the bridegroom is Ibrahim Qutb Shah, flanked by the local Qazi and the elders.

As the light brightens on the stage, we hear Arabic passages being recited softly. We start with the Bijapur section.

QAZI: Sultan Hussain Nizam Shah, it has been resolved that your daughter, Shahzadi Chand Bibi, should be given in nikkah to Sultan Ali Adil Shah. May we start the proceedings?

NIZAM SHAH: Yes, you may.

QAZI (*addressing the gathering*): It has been resolved to hand over in nikkah Shahzadi Chand Bibi, daughter of Sultan Hussain Nizam Shah to Sultan Ali Adil Shah.

(*Turns to Ali Adil Shah.*)

Sultan Ali Adil Shah, is this relationship acceptable to you?

ADIL SHAH: Yes, it is acceptable.

QAZI: Is it acceptable to you?

ADIL SHAH: Yes, it is acceptable.

QAZI: Is it acceptable to you?

ADIL SHAH: Yes, it is acceptable.

(*The Qazi then moves to the chilman and addresses the bride sitting behind it.*)

QAZI: Shahzadi Chand Bibi, daughter of Sultan Hussain Nizam Shah, it is resolved to unite you in nikkah with Sultan Ali Adil Shah. Is this relationship acceptable to you?

CHAND BIBI: Yes, it is acceptable.

(*As the exchange is repeated three times, the scene shifts to the right of the stage, where the Qazi of Golconda is addressing the elders.*)

QAZI: It has been resolved that Shahzadi Bibi Jamaal, daughter of Sultan Hussain Nizam Shah of Ahmadnagar, should be joined in nikkah with Sultan Ibrahim Qutb Shah.

(*addressing Qutb Shah*) Sultan Ibrahim Qutb Shah, it has been resolved that Shahzadi Bibi Jamaal, daughter of Sultan Hussain Nizam Shah, should be given in nikkah to you. Is this bond acceptable to you?

QUTB SHAH: Yes, it is acceptable.

(*As this exchange is repeated three times, the lights fade out.*)

SCENE EIGHT

The Palace in Vijayanagara

Ramaraya, Venkatadri, and Tirumala Raya in conference. They are laughing.

RAMARAYA: So the great weddings have taken place! Weddings? They are not really weddings in the eyes of God, you know. The Turukas are practical. Not sacraments but contracts. Convenient agreements.

VENKATADRI: No question of a bond extending over all future births.

RAMARAYA: Tirumala, ask Nizam Shah why we weren't invited. Ask him not to be too complacent. He may still need our men to help his new sons-in-law in their marital beds.

VENKATADRI: We could at least have sent some *prasad* from Tirupati.

TIRUMALA: You should ask your farzand, Brother, that Adil Shah. It's not very courteous of him not to invite you.

RAMARAYA: As soon as I heard of his betrothal to Nizam Shah's daughter, I sent word. 'Beware,' I said, 'This is dangerous territory. Don't you know Nizam Shah is a sworn enemy of mine?'

VENKATADRI: Of course, he knows. They all know what all this means.

RAMARAYA: And you know the reply he sent? 'May the dust of your feet be on the crown of our heads. I sincerely believe this relationship will strengthen all our relationships in the Deccan.'

VENKATADRI: Arrogance.

TIRUMALA: Sheer arrogance.

VENKATADRI: Qutb hasn't even replied, has he?

TIRUMALA: He was always a coward. Pusillanimous. Ten years he spent in this palace licking our mattresses. Eating our leavings. Salivating. All that must have worn his tongue threadbare.

RAMARAYA (*suddenly serious*): But these weddings are not merely the signing of contracts. The two new sons-in-law are a proclamation that Nizam Shah means business. That's clear to them. Clear to us. So they are getting together. Good, so some preliminary precautions may be in order.

VENKATADRI: Yes, Brother.

RAMARAYA: Tirumala, you start with twenty thousand cavalry, five hundred elephants, and fifty thousand infantry immediately. Alert the security on the banks of River Krishna. We should not let them cross over to the southern side. Block them at every step. Erect earthen mounds along the southern banks of the river. Control every ford on the stream, every crossing. Build mud forts to prevent entry wherever possible.

TIRUMALA: I shall have the smaller cannons mounted on them.

(*A maid enters.*)

MAID: The Queen is here, sir.

RAMARAYA (*taken aback*): The Queen? What's she doing here in the men's enclave? Tell her we'll come to the chandrashala.

MAID: She's already here, sir.

(*Satyabhama enters. The maid withdraws.*)

RAMARAYA: What're you doing here?

VENKATADRI: If you'd informed us, we would've come to the chandrashala ourselves, Sister-in-Law.

SATYABHAMA: The chandrashala is a sieve. Every word spoken there leaks into the market place. I wanted to talk to you—just the three of you.

(*She is obviously nervous.*)

VENKATADRI: Please, sit down, Sister-in-Law. Relax.

(*She sits. A long pause.*)

RAMARAYA (*almost brusquely*): Yes?

SATYABHAMA: Is it true the four Turuka Sultans have combined against us? Including Adil Shah?

VENKATADRI: Yes, sad. But true.

SATYABHAMA: So there'll be war?

TIRUMALA: Yes, Sister-in-Law. They obviously mean war. And a big one.

SATYABHAMA (*nervous, almost mumbling*): And may I know who'll lead our forces?

VENKATADRI (*jumping in before anyone else replies*): We're just coming to that.

TIRUMALA: In the past we faced each Sultan singly. We crushed them like bedbugs. Now they're combining forces. And challenging us. It's a major operation now. At least they're trying to show that it's going to be a major operation. A lot of show! Not worrisome but grand, nevertheless.

VENKATADRI (*trying to soothe her fears*): It's a huge army although much smaller than ours. We shall stretch our men along the banks of Krishna. Like a net. We have to be in charge at several points. So we were about to suggest to Brother that perhaps Tirumala and I could lead the operations jointly this time.

SATYABHAMA (*relieved*): May God grant you success. I haven't slept for nights now since I heard the news. I came to ask you if it was possible for you two to do just that—to take over the lead this time. His health isn't well…

RAMARAYA (*expressionless*): So you two want to share the command this time?

SATYABHAMA (*sensing his mood*): Now, please, don't say no. That's what I've come to ask too. Let them lead. It's what we all want. (*To her brothers-in-law*) I am so relieved. That's all I wanted to know.

VENKATADRI: We'll be guided by you of course, Brother. But we'll be at the front and follow the guidelines you set up for us. You rest in the capital.

RAMARAYA: So you destroy the Turukas on the battlefield while I sit here, in the capital, scratching my bottom?

TIRUMALA: It's not like that at all, Brother. Your presence here's enough to numb the enemies. Everyone's aware of that. But this time there are four of them together and it's going to be a demanding operation.

RAMARAYA (*slowly getting excited*): That's precisely it. This is not like the previous encounters—mere skirmishes we joined in by choice on behalf of some footling Sultan. This time they're challenging *me*. I'm being recognized as Vijayanagara incarnate, as the Tuluva royal family has never recognized me. All my life I've been humiliated by the progeny of Krishna Raya, *her* royal relatives—

SATYABHAMA (*upset, to the brothers-in-law*): He always does that. The moment he gets upset he takes it out on my father.

RAMARAYA: It rankles, don't you know? The nomenclature. 'Aliya'. The Son-in-Law. Hired to be the Son-in-Law.

SATYABHAMA: How can you be so vicious? We've been married sixty years now. We've had four children who're of Aravidu blood. My father admired your courage, your capabilities and gave me in marriage to you. He gave my sister in marriage to (*pointing to Venkatadri*) Brother-in-Law. Sixty years ago!

RAMARAYA: Me, Venkatadri here, Tirumala—we are Aravidus. We are of the great Chalukya lineage and yet we are not good enough for her royal relatives. What've we been doing all these decades? Playing watchdogs for the Tuluva marionette plonked on the throne. You talk of your father making us his sons-in-law. Well, by doing so he managed to ensure there will be lifelong guards for his royal family, didn't he? It was a stroke of genius.

VENKATADRI: Brother, what's the point of bringing all that up now? Let's not upset Sister-in-Law with it.

SATYABHAMA: This is why I despair of opening my mouth. He suddenly gets excited and launches a tirade of these absurd accusations. These grievances of long ago—they just erupt out of the blue. But it was not like that at all. My poor father loved him. It's not his fault that his family joined up with the courtiers to foil his intentions.

RAMARAYA: Of course, your generous, loving relations! For twenty years I have played their game. Now I shall take over. The entire horde of Krishna Raya's enemies coming together—not against Vijayanagara. Not against Krishna Raya's family, but me. Aravidu Ramaraya. It's an omen from heaven. For the Chalukya lineage to assert itself. No more Aliya Ramaraya! 'Ramaraya, the Son-in-Law' is dead.

SATYABHAMA (*agitated*): Please, please, don't say such inauspicious things. They're *apa-shakuna*. If you want to go to the battlefield, go. But don't say these evil things.

RAMARAYA: Yes, and it's time for a new *yuga*. The yuga of Chalukyas. You know, once I was in Tirupati, in conference with the *sthanapatis* of the Nayaks of Madurai, Tanjavuru, Ikkeri, Gingi, and Mysuru. The place was packed to suffocation with pilgrims, and we had to conduct our secret negotiations, closeted in a tiny room.

SATYABHAMA (*suddenly gets up*): I can't take this. Why're we raking that up?

RAMARAYA (*ignoring her*): Our negotiations were secret and important. It was a tense argument. And suddenly I wanted to urinate. I tried to control my bladder…

SATYABHAMA: I'm going. (*Turning to Tirumala and Venkatadri*) Please, please, I beg of you. Don't let him…

(*She rushes out. Tirumala and Venkatadri half get up to see her out, but stop non-plussed as Ramaraya continues. They too have heard the story before.*)

RAMARAYA (*laughs*): Satyabhama knows this story. I've told it to her. Several times. It's not the story she hates as much as the conclusion I draw from it. Our negotiations were secret and important. I had to piss but the discussions wouldn't end. There was no way I could leave. The crowds made it impossible for me to move, and then there was the fear that the sthanapatis may feel insulted if I left. I couldn't stop my bladder from dribbling. My thighs under my dress were getting wet. The stench almost began to buffet me. Not just me. I could see from their faces that everyone there could smell the piss. The place reeked with it. But they were royal ambassadors. They sat there stone-faced and pretended to focus on what I was saying.

This reputation of mine as 'Son-in-law of Krishna Raya', 'Aliya Ramaraya'—the protector of Vijayanagara, but don't-come-near-the throne, thank you—it's just like that stink. It attacks everyone's nose but no one admits to smelling it.

Do you know what these Sultans are doing now? They are providing me with the opportunity to wipe out that stink. They're helping me prove I can decimate the lot in one fell swoop. I shall clean up the land and what'll rise from it is not Vijayanagara but something greater—I'm not fighting for Vijayanagara now—I'm fighting for Aravidu glory. These Sultans are the agents of my destiny. They are providing me with a test of the glory of our lineage.

(*He is excited. He stands up as though addressing a huge audience.*)

Venkatadri, Tirumala, inform the Sultans. Inform our public. Inform our tributaries, our generals, and dependancies. What faces me now is Kurukshetra. A new age will emerge out of this encounter. I am Partha, the Supreme King of the Aravidu clan, the returning scion of the Chalukyas. Let's welcome the New Age! To Chalukya glory!

SCENE NINE

Outskirts of Bijapur

The four Sultans in a tent on a carpet with piles of different species of mangoes in front of them. Mango tasting is in progress. Hakim Qasim Beg waits in a corner. The whole air is vibrant with anticipation and daring. Only Nizam Shah looks a little apprehensive.

The Sultans wash their hands, wipe their lips. The plates are removed by the servants.

BARID SHAH: *Wah, wah*! *Bohot khoob*!

QUTB SHAH: We must confess that we had never come across this flavour in mangoes before. 'Divine' is the only adjective that comes to mind. And that's no exaggeration. Reminds you of wild honey but with the slightest touch of tamarind—just enough to excite the tongue—without spoiling its sweetness. What family is it?

BARID SHAH: If it's the result of grafting, I must say your mango expert deserves to be specially honoured.

ADIL SHAH (*happy*): Absolutely no tampering with nature. They're a genuine local variety. Not much known. But simple and honest in taste. Genuine in colour. Like everything else here in Bijapur.

(*Laughter.*)

NIZAM SHAH: Shall we then talk genuinely?

(*The laughter fades. They become serious.*)

BARID SHAH: Yes, let us.

(*Pause.*)

ADIL SHAH: Let me be explicit then. If we mean to cause any kind of harm to Vijayanagar, I am not with you.

BARID SHAH: Bravo! With such a resounding opening pronouncement, what more can we ask for? So comforting. We meet here in an effort to control Ramaraya's shenanigans. And we start with a statement calculated to buoy up our spirits. Our host says he is not with the rest of us!

ADIL SHAH: Ali Barid, you know perfectly well I have publicly called Ramaraya my father. I've placed him on that pedestal of my own free will, under no duress, my submission witnessed by the entire population of Vijayanagar. I have been helped by him again and again—whenever I called for it. His wife has welcomed me as 'farzand'. I am not prepared to betray their love and trust.

BARID SHAH: So why are we here? Sultan Nizam Shah, you've brought us here. What for? Your Son-in-Law number one has clearly declared his loyalties. What about the other Badshah?

(*He waves to Qutb Shah, who does not respond. He merely smiles and shrugs.*)

NIZAM SHAH: We four have always had our differences of opinion about our territories. But since Ramaraya came on the scene, he has turned it into an endless game, pitting us against each other. The world is laughing at us. Unless we come together, we'll continue to be made monkeys of by him.

ADIL SHAH: And whose fault is it? It's we who've been spreading out the carpet for him—inviting him in to sort out our squabbles.

BARID SHAH: Will that script now change? Do you see a future where we all agree not to fight amongst ourselves, indeed embrace each other—if only to keep Ramaraya out of the picture. Map, rather. Everlasting peace among the Sultans! Is that a realistic expectation? We agree to return all the regions we have grabbed from each other?

(*They snigger in embarrassment. Only Nizam Shah remains unsmiling.*)

NIZAM SHAH: So you see, the very notion of amity and peace between us is cause enough for levity. Yes, I have invited you all here. We have to do something. But I am unable to suggest the next step.

BARID SHAH: Forgive me for pointing out that the first invitation to Ramaraya to provide succour came from Sultan Nizam Shah. When Ali Adil Shah's father started losing his sanity and started creating havoc, it was the Honourable Sultan who asked Ramaraya's help and dragged us all into the mess. He tasted blood and has become addicted. We agree to put on a show, he pulls the strings. We squabble, he laughs.

NIZAM SHAH: So my first plea is: Let's forget the past. Yes, I plead guilty. I have indulged in that game myself. I beg your pardon. Please let us not try to analyze those unfortunate accusations and counter-accusations. You said this. So I said this. You could've said something else. And so on. Let's unite and decide on a course of action, more mature, more beneficial to us all.

BARID SHAH: Let me then start off by stating why I'm here. Ramaraya has been willfully offending me in various ways and I have tolerated him. But Jahangir Khan was my man. An innocent officer who loyally followed my orders. Ramaraya had absolutely no reason to kill him. No right. I shall never be forgiven by my people if I accept that insult.

QUTB SHAH: I must say. His viciousness was totally uncalled for.

(*They nod in agreement.*)

BARID SHAH: We must of course keep in mind another aspect. He provides shelter to every aspiring traitor in one's court. Many planning to assassinate me tomorrow may be sharpening their daggers on his whetstone today.

ADIL SHAH (*smiles*): You want to blame him for conspiracies in our court? Not fair.

QUTB SHAH: There would be fewer murderous plans hatched if Vijayanagar was not so conveniently across the border.

ADIL SHAH (*ironic*): As for example—

QUTB SHAH (*smiling*): For example, myself. If Ramaraya hadn't given me sanctuary, my brother would've finished me off.

BARID SHAH: He's been crafty. But where's all this leading us? Adil Shah, let's stop beating about the bush. What concrete suggestion do you have?

ADIL SHAH: I cannot forget that when my father was going berserk—when he died—it was Ramaraya who came to my aid. Not one of you made a move. It's hard to forget.

NIZAM SHAH (*exasperated*): Can't we forget old grievances and make a fresh start?

ADIL SHAH: But I agree he's becoming arrogant. Overbearing. In the last several months he has never missed a chance to snub me by pointing out what I owe him. It had started right at the beginning, of course. When he was returning home after sending me the keys of Kalyan, he casually took over the forts of Udgir and Bagalkot. When I sought an explanation, he didn't even meet my messenger. And then he drives me beyond endurance warning me not to accept the hand of Shahzadi Chand Bibi. 'Remember, marrying my enemy's daughter will make you my enemy.' The intent was clear. 'I shall be in charge of your personal life too henceforth.' That I will not accept.

QUTB SHAH: I've been putting up with his insolence all these years. But there's a limit. Six months ago, his men marched through my realm without informing me. And then created a rumpus in Koilkonda and Guntur. Desecrated the mosques there. Ransacked several of my villages. Why? This has never happened before in the Deccan. There was absolutely no reason to be so bloody-minded except to cock a snook at me. But I agree with Adil Shah. Ramaraya has been a help in the past.

ADIL SHAH: Let's cut him down to size. That's all that's required.

BARID SHAH: And how do we do that?

ADIL SHAH: I've thought about it. We tell him, in future we'll not have him cross the Krishna river. He sticks to the south of the river, we stick to the north.

BARID SHAH: Ah, well. I see two problems right away.

ADIL SHAH (*laughs*): I see four—the four sitting here.

BARID SHAH (*ignoring him*): First, he is used to dictating the terms. If we state ours first, he'll see it as an affront. He'll simply refuse to negotiate. Then, secondly, he'll think we're only trying to cut him off from his beloved Kalyan.

NIZAM SHAH: He'll rear up at the mere suggestion. That's true.

ADIL SHAH: Leave it to me. I'll tackle him. I think he'll listen to me.

(*Cynical laughter from Barid Shah.*)

BARID SHAH: May God grant the brute the wisdom to do so. But we must prepare for the worst. First, we would like Sultan Nizam Shah's two respected sons-in-law to set our minds at rest. You will participate in the battle against Vijayanagar, if necessary. Will you or won't you?

QUTB SHAH: Come on. Surely, we wouldn't be here now if that was not a given?

ADIL SHAH: Ready for the wedding. Ready for the battle.

(*Laughter.*)

I shall talk to him.

BARID SHAH: All that's fine. But that leads us to the next consideration. To cross the Krishna river, we have to march through Bijapur territory. Adil Shah, please inform your forces that we're here as friends this time. Not enemies as usual. If your men get the signals mixed up, the results could be disastrous.

ADIL SHAH: Please, be assured I shall inform my forces that you're coming to settle political issues and not family matters, so there's no need for lethal weapons.

(*Laughter.*)

Please come, be relaxed, taste the hospitality of Bijapur.

(*Hakim Qasim Beg gets up and comes to Nizam Shah with his medications.*)

NIZAM SHAH: Ah, Hazrat Hakim Sahib! No escaping his attentions. My medication.

(*He gets up. Barid Shah and Qutb Shah get up to leave with him.*)

ADIL SHAH: Some Sufi saints from Kashmir have come to our *khanqa*. They bring with them some mystic music, rooted in Persia. *Sufiana Qalam*. If you're so inclined, you're welcome to attend their session for a while.

(*They depart talking.*)

SCENE TEN

The Vijayanagara Palace

Ramaraya and Tirumalamba. She blesses him with an arati and flowers and jewellery. Satyabhama waits at the side.

RAMARAYA: Mother, the four Sultans from the north have united and decided to attack our empire. Your blessings and the benediction of our Family Deity have ensured that we've never lacked in anything.

TIRUMALAMBA: You're a great king. And until now, our neighbours had acted in good faith and honour as befits their station. Time has led them astray. I don't know the pros and cons of the situation. You are a child still, Ramu. Do you need to face such a hostile situation? It seems to me that it would be advisable for you to ensure peace by attending to the demands of time.

RAMARAYA: I shouldn't be concerned, mother. They are in the palm of my hand and have until now been content to live in the space allotted to them. It's beneath my dignity to deal or negotiate with them. It's beneath your dignity which is important, for you are the Queen Mother of the Chalukya realm. I shall decimate them in no time. Just watch.

TIRUMALAMBA: May victory be yours.

(He moves to his wife Satyabhama who puts kumkum on his forehead and silently touches his feet. He goes away.)

Nizam Shah's Camp

RUMI KHAN: Sultan, the Hindus have made it impossible for us to cross the river by erecting a solid human wall on the bank of the river. Their army has been stationed shoulder to shoulder, all gaps blocked, all fords secured.

NIZAM SHAH: Of course, they anticipated our moves and planned the blockade weeks ahead, Rumi Khan. What did you expect? But this is not going to be a stationary confrontation. That's the last thing we should allow to happen. Move up and down along the bank. Inspect the possibility of a crack over a distance of every four *kos* and keep expert swimmers ready. Mobility—that's of the essence.

RUMI KHAN: Don't worry, sir. We shall find a breach.

NIZAM SHAH: But Rumi Khan, don't get carried away. Our crossing is just a feint. It's to keep their army pinned down on their side. Remember, the battle has to take place on *our* side of the river. It must. Always. Keep the cannons movable on the north bank, ready for action.

RUMI KHAN (*laughs*): We tempt them across and blast them. Is that right?

NIZAM SHAH: He's dying to assert his right to cross north. That's his weak spot. He'll rise to the bait.

The Vijayanagara Camp

TIRUMALA: It's a disaster, Brother. The Turukas have crossed the river.

VENKATADRI: How did that happen? How did you let it happen, you fools? And where?

TIRUMALA: Apparently near Talikota.

VENKATADRI: You bloody eunuchs, what were our soldiers doing then? The crossings've been blocked for over three weeks now. How did you let it happen?

TIRUMALA: The Turukas kept moving along the northern bank and we moved along with them. Their cavalry moved ahead and we kept them within our sights. Then suddenly without warning their cavalry turned back and raced to a crossing point they'd chosen. Our elephants couldn't keep pace, Brother. You know how it is. By the time we had arrived with our elephants, they had crossed the river.

VENKATADRI: Incompetent bastards! What shit do you eat for food?

NARASIMHA: More than a thousand elephants, sir. And we had orders to stick close to them. It was impossible to move parallelly with the Arab horses. We did our best. But it was not possible.

Nizam Shah's Camp

NIZAM SHAH: Dilawar, we shall strike camp here. Here we'll face our fate, God willing. Name our four standards, write the names of the twelve Imams on them and plant them here in a row.

Rumi Khan, what about the cannons? Are they in position?

RUMI KHAN: We moved them ahead of the entire infantry. It was a huge risk but it worked. Of our six hundred cannons, the bigger ones will be stationed in the first row, with the medium and the smaller ones in rows behind them.

NIZAM SHAH: Are you sure we'll be able to face the onslaught of elephants?

RUMI KHAN: We'll chain the cannons together next to one another so the elephants can't pass through.

NIZAM SHAH (*dubious*): You think it'll work?

RUMI KHAN: I've seen the deployment in Istanbul. It can make for an unbreachable barricade, God willing.

(*Explosions begin in the background along with much shouting and screaming.*)

SCENE ELEVEN

The Vijayanagara Camp

Ramaraya with his entourage. He is not particularly excited and supervises the arrangements with great calm and confidence.

RAMARAYA: How are the Turuka forces arranged, Bisilappa?

BISILAPPA: Barid Shah and Qutb Shah are on the left.

RAMARAYA: Good. Strike my tent here. I must face Nizam Shah. My pearl throne is to be on a height so everyone can see me.

BISILAPPA: Adil Shah is camping on the right.

RAMARAYA (*laughs*): He didn't want to join battle. What's he doing here? Bored with his wife already?

BISILAPPA: There doesn't seem to be much enthusiasm in his camp, it's true. They're taking it easy. Nizam Shah has planted his flag exactly between the two camps.

RAMARAYA: Plant my battle pillar right in front of him. I'll be here. Anyone who crosses the line of this battle pillar will retreat only at the peril of losing his head. Has our armoury arrived intact? All the weaponry's here?

BISILAPPA: No fears, master. We have a thousand cannons ready—and fifty thousand matchlocks.

RAMARAYA: What about the elephants? Are they well fed? Mahouts well groomed?

BISILAPPA: We've two thousand war elephants, sir. We shall overwhelm the enemy.

(*A messenger comes rushing in.*)

MESSENGER: Sir, bad news. The right flank of our army has walked into a trap and is getting decimated.

BISILAPPA: What happened?

MESSENGER: Their archers attacked us and we confronted them and pushed them back. They retreated, we pursued them, when suddenly they opened up their front row. They had cleverly concealed their cannons behind the men and the moment the front line parted, they started bombarding us—not with cannon balls, sir, we were prepared for that—with metal coins. Sharp-edged metal coins. They cut through our men. It was a shower of death, sir. A bloodbath. The general says at least five thousand have been killed.

RAMARAYA: And we had no information of the set-up? What were our agents doing? Tiruvengala Nayaka, where are our cannons? Push them ahead.

BISILAPPA: Yellappa Nayaka, run and see what's happened.

(*Yellappa Nayaka runs. Another messenger comes running.*)

MESSENGER: Tragedy, sir! An arrow has pierced the right eye of Danda Nayaka Tirumala. He's completely blinded and bleeding. He's left the battleground and returned to his tent. His forces are losing heart without him.

RAMARAYA: The fool! The bloody idiot. And he wanted to lead the army! Lily-livered wimp! He doesn't have to desert the field if his eye is wounded. He can surely continue to lead the men with one eye shut. And where's Venkatadri?

BISILAPPA: He was in hot pursuit of Barid Shah's contingent. He chased them behind the hillock.

RAMARAYA: They've both got to be here for Goodness' sake. Our men can't go on without someone to direct them. Bring my palanquin! Bring my palanquin! I must lead my men. My men need me to lead them.

BISILAPPA: Please, sir. Don't go into the battlefield. We've able leaders there—Kodanda Nayaka, Kalinga Nayaka. They'll handle any crisis.

RAMARAYA (*excited*): Then why am I here? I could've been resting back home. My brave dauntless men need to see with their own eyes that I am with them. I am their leader. Where's my palanquin? Where's my palanquin?

BISILAPPA: Not a palanquin. No, sir. Let's ride. Horses are easier to manoeuvre. Please listen to us.

RAMARAYA (*laughs*): Don't be an imbecile, Bisilappa Nayaka. Why do I need a horse? Manoeuvre it? Ha. I am not planning to run away. I want to lead my loyal forces. My brave men. I want to be amidst them as they fight for me. For *my* glory.

(*He is excited now and shouting.*)

Where are the litters of *baksheesh*? Precious stones? Gold coins? Jewellery? Bring them. Bring them all here.

(*As he climbs into his palanquin, servants bring large plates heaped with valuables and other presents next to him. He snatches fistfuls of jewellery which he flings into the fighting mob.*)

There, there, warriors of Vijayanagara. Take this. This wealth—priceless gems, choicest jewels—these are all yours to take. You've earned them. Go on. Take my palanquin forward. Hurry.

BISILAPPA: Sir, sir. Fierce fighting is going on in that area. Please don't go there. It's hazardous.

RAMARAYA: Hazard? What hazard? I have led these men for forty years. Forty years of victory. The Turukas are men of straw—we'll blow them away—I'll unleash energy into you—create fountains of energy in you. See how I'll bring out the men in you. I sweep down on the enemies like an eagle on curling snakes. Garuda—Garuda—

(*He flings the gifts at the soldiers like one possessed.*)

Fight. Fight for the glory of the Aravidu dynasty. For the honour of Kalyana Chalukyas. Here I come. Garuda.

(*He is enraptured. Flinging jewellery to his soldiers, calling out to them, united with them in an almost mystical relationship, he is in a state of euphoria as his palanquin lurches forward.*)

SCENE TWELVE

Adil Shah's Camp

SARDAR: Sultan, Venkatadri has rounded the tower hillock and attacked Barid Shah's forces from the rear, taking them by surprise. They're badly trapped. But we can relieve them by attacking them from the right. Otherwise they're finished.

ADIL SHAH (*anguished*): But I've promised Ramaraya my forces won't fight. We shouldn't move from here. It's a word of honour.

SARDAR (*excited*): But Barid Shah's men are being cut to pieces. Our only chance of helping them is to jump in from the right. Now. Please sir. Venkatadri's attack can be deflected but we can't wait. Now, sir, now. Please.

ADIL SHAH: But ... but ...

SARDAR: Venkatadri's men are not expecting us to attack. That's clear from the way they're marching with their backs to us. We couldn't have asked for a more perfect position.

(*Adil Shah hesitates.*)

Sir, don't you remember how Venkatadri humiliated you at Kalyan? You swore vengeance then. Have you forgotten? This is the moment, sir—

ADIL SHAH (*in despair*): All right. Attack.

(*At the signal from the Sardar, Adil Shah's men plunge into the turmoil.*)

SARDAR (*smiles*): One can't jump into the stream and not swim.

SCENE THIRTEEN

Nizam Shah's Camp

A messenger comes running.

MESSENGER: Sultan, Our right flank is collapsing. The Hindu infantrymen are fighting like demons and their archers are deadly. Qutb Shah and Barid Shah have both sent word that they're retreating. They're finding it difficult to face the onslaught.

NIZAM SHAH: Where's Obaid Khan? Ask him to use the cannons to bombard the enemy. Tell the general whatever happens we're not to lose the high grounds by the river corner. Where's Adil Shah? He was meant to support Barid. Has he let us down? (*In distress*) Has the bastard really let us down?

(*Rumi Khan enters excited, shouting. He pulls Nizam Shah by his arm.*)

RUMI KHAN: Sultan, Sultan. Look what we've here. A gift from God.

NIZAM SHAH: What're you shouting for? Can't you see I'm busy here? The news is bad—

RUMI KHAN: Sultan, you won't believe it if you don't see it with your own eyes.

(*Nizam Shah turns on Rumi Khan, exasperated. At a sign from Rumi Khan, a litter is carried in. Ramaraya is sitting in it, fatigued and listless. The litter is lowered in front of Nizam Shah, who is flabbergasted to see Ramaraya in person in front of him. Rumi Khan laughs triumphantly. There's commotion as the other generals and soldiers in the camp realize Ramaraya has been captured and brought in. Rumi Khan raises his hand and silences them, while Nizam Shah seems mesmerized by his captive and barely seems to be responding to Rumi Khan's account.*)

RUMI KHAN: It was Zafer. I'd asked him to get on the elephant Ghulam Ali and charge into the enemy forces. He saw the palanquin from far—a royal palanquin being tossed around by bearers in the middle of the maelstrom. He couldn't see who it was, so asked the mahout to take Ghulam Ali to the spot. The bearers got scared by the elephant and dropped the palanquin and fled. This revered old man was rolling helplessly on the ground and a Brahmin next to him was shouting, 'Don't hurt him. Don't strike him. It's the King of Vijayanagar!' If the fool hadn't started hollering like that perhaps Zafer would have gone on. But now of course he stopped and picked up the King and brought him to me. He didn't believe it was the King …

(*By now Nizam Shah has found his tongue.*)

NIZAM SHAH: But … but … the Suratrana himself? You should be in your camp, sir. What are you doing here in this melee?

(*Ramaraya is limp with exhaustion and humiliation. His voice is so low he can barely be heard.*)

RAMARAYA: Where's Adil Shah? Please send me to Adil Shah's camp.

NIZAM SHAH (*fully awake*): Of course, I'd forgotten. Your dear farzand. My dear Son-in-Law!

(*Waves to an attendant.*)

Inform Sultan Adil Shah that the Suratrana of Vijayanagar awaits his arrival in our camp. Ramaraya himself in the tent of Sultan Nizam Shah! I can't believe it! Dear God! (*To Ramaraya*) How come you're here, sir? You should be in your camp with your generals.

(*Ramaraya is slowly recovering his courage. He smiles. He runs his forefinger across his forehead as though to say, 'It's fate.'*)

Your presence fills us with wonder, sir. And admiration. Such energy at your age. Such self-confidence.

RAMARAYA: What am I to be scared of, Sultan? You've been in the same position in the past, more than once—my prisoner after losing a battle—and I've sent you home with full royal honours. I've not the least doubt that you'll show the same courtesy to me.

NIZAM SHAH (*almost to himself*): I should've arranged for some paan. How stupid of me!

RAMARAYA: Let Adil Shah come. I'll go with him. You others return to your homes. Victorious. I grant you. This time victory is yours.

(*Nizam Shah murmurs to himself in answer. Ramaraya is slowly becoming more confident.*)

There are four of you this time. And I have bungled and, therefore, must pay a heavier price. I shall do so. I'll reward you amply. Where's Adil Shah? He's taking a long time. He'd said he would come if I sent for him.

NIZAM SHAH: Your favourite son's on his way. So, while we wait for him, let me tell you a secret.

RAMARAYA: A secret on a battlefield?

NIZAM SHAH: Quite. And the whole world already knows the secret. (*Points to Hakim Qasim Beg*) You don't know this man. Hakim Qasim Beg. He attends to me. He is a pest. He is always with me because my begum believes that so long as he's with me, I'll not die, I'll be fine. But the truth of the matter is I am dying. A disease is eating away at my insides—chewing them insidiously. It's been spreading for a long time. But now I'm told it may be a matter of—a few weeks? God alone knows. I don't. The Hakim doesn't.

RAMARAYA: At any other time, I would've asked you to come to Hampi for treatment. We have the best doctors in the world. Ayurvedic. Yunani. Chinese. Even now the Sultan would be most welcome once the dust has settled here. It's a royal invitation.

NIZAM SHAH: Thank you. You're most kind. But I have to return to Ahmadnagar. My begum will be waiting for me. (*To an attendant*) A drink for the Suratrana.

(*While the drink is brought, Nizam Shah begins to murmur, which doesn't bother Ramaraya, since he is not even listening. Nizam Shah quickly confabulates with Rumi Khan and Hakim, and then continues.*)

How many years has it been since I started dreaming this dream! I must defeat Ramaraya. How many since I started fantasizing this event. And it's here. Just the two of us! No one else to spoil the intimacy. Just the two of us. You and me. God!

RAMARAYA: Is Adil Shah coming?

NIZAM SHAH: I am dying, Suratrana, and you've completely messed up my death. You've created such a terrible conundrum for me. Is there any point in killing you now? To let you go alive—that would be a greater revenge. A vanquished Ramaraya. The undefeatable, in chains! Such triumph. Almighty God, for years I have been banging my head against the wall in an effort to decide what I should do at the most important moment in my life. And now you haven't left me even enough time to think it out.

(*almost crying out aloud*) Why do I have to be confused at this moment? You should've been here, Begum. Why aren't you here? Begum!

(*He launches into a silent dialogue with the invisible Begum. Ramaraya is too absorbed in his plight to pay attention, while the Hakim who is obviously used to this occurrence watches, worried and tense, occasionally looking away to see if Adil Shah has arrived. He gets a signal that Adil Shah has come.*)

HAKIM: Sultan Adil Shah is here. Enough now, *Huzoor*. This is no time for pleasantries.

RAMARAYA (*gets up in sheer joy*): Ah, farzand. You've come. You haven't let me down.

ADIL SHAH: Appa-ji, how did you get into this mess?

(*He moves towards Ramaraya. But at a signal from Rumi Khan, two guards step forward and block Adil Shah's way and stop him, without of course physically restraining him. Adil Shah, baffled, looks at Nizam Shah. Rumi Khan pulls out his sword, when Adil Shah realizes what's happening.*)

ADIL SHAH: No! Don't! Please.

(*Nizam Shah stands frozen and the Hakim shouts out.*)

HAKIM: If you hesitate now, Huzoor, this pestilence will spread and destroy us all.

(*Nizam Shah signals to Rumi Khan who with one swing of the sword beheads Ramaraya.*)

ADIL SHAH (*screams*): How can you do this? He's our guest.

(*He rushes to Ramaraya and crouches sobbing loudly near Ramaraya's body.*)

NIZAM SHAH: May God forgive me if I have done wrong.

(*At a sign from him, Rumi Khan brings a spear and impales Ramaraya's head on it.*)

Take this to Kashi to wash it of its sins! And here's my dowry to you, Adil Shah. The Deccan! The whole of Deccan!

(*Rumi Khan takes up the grisly trophy and displays it all round. Soldiers rush in and raise Nizam Shah on their shoulders, carry him away. Rumi Khan plants the impaled head in front of Adil Shah, who sits crouched in misery. The shouts and screams increase until the noise is deafening and becomes continuous with the sound track of Scene Two. The flow of celebrating soldiers conceals both the severed head and Adil Shah from view. The stage darkens, the noise subsides until there is total silence. Lights come on onstage to show the rocky terrain around Vijayanagara. We are back at the beginning of Scene One.*)

BIBLIOGRAPHY

English Texts

Eaton, Richard M. *A Social History of the Deccan, 1300–1761: Eight Indian Lives*, Cambridge: Cambridge University Press, 2005.

Eaton, Richard M. and Phillip Wagoner. *Power, Memory, Architecture, 1300–1800*. New Delhi: Oxford University Press, 2014.

Fritz, John M. and George Mitchell (ed.). *New Light on Hampi*. Mumbai: Marg, 2001.

Sewell, Robert. *A Forgotten Empire, Vijayanagara*. New Delhi: Publications Division, (1900), 1962.

Stein, Burton. *Vijayanagara*. Cambridge: Cambridge University Press, 1993.

Kannada Texts

Adilshahi Sahitya, Vol 1-18. Commissioned by Krishna Kolhar Kulkarni. Vijayapura: F. G. Halikatti Samshodhana Kendra, 2014–18.

Lakshman Telgavi (ed.). *Ramaji Tirumala Harikareya 'Ramarajana Bakhairu'*. Hampi: Prasaranga, Kannada University, 2011.

ABOUT THE PLAYWRIGHT

Girish Karnad is a playwright, film-maker, and actor. He writes in Kannada, the language of the state of Karnataka, and has translated his plays into English. Some of his more recent plays, however, were written originally in English. His plays have been performed in most Indian languages as well as abroad.

He graduated from Karnatak University, Dharwad, in mathematics (1958) and was a Rhodes Scholar at Oxford University where he received an MA in philosophy, politics, and economics (1963).

After working with Oxford University Press, India, as editor, he resigned to freelance, and was awarded the Homi Bhabha Fellowship for creative writing. He used this opportunity to explore techniques of traditional theatre forms and write *Hayavadana*, which initiated a new movement in Indian theatre.

Subsequently, he went on to serve in cultural institutions of national importance: as the Director of the Film and Television Institute of India, Pune, the Chairman of the Sangeet Natak Akademi (the National Academy of the Performing Arts), New Delhi, and the Director of the Nehru Centre, Indian High Commission, London.

While he was at the University of Chicago as visiting professor and Fulbright-Playwright-in-Residence, he wrote *Nāga-Mandala*. The play was premiered in the USA by the Guthrie Theatre, Minneapolis, which then commissioned him to write *The Fire and the Rain*.

The Haymarket Theatre, Leicester, UK, commissioned and premiered *Bali: The Sacrifice*. His radio play, *The Dreams of Tipu Sultan*, was commissioned by BBC, London, and broadcast on the fiftieth anniversary of Indian Independence. He further celebrated the occasion by directing *Swarajnama*, a television programme in thirteen episodes on India's struggle for independence, for Doordarshan.

He wrote and presented the telefilm *The Bhagavad Gita* as part of the programme *Art That Shook the World* for BBC Two (2002). He provided the voice of A.P.J. Abdul Kalam, former President of India, in the audiobook version of Kalam's autobiography *Wings of Fire*.

His plays have been produced by most of the major directors in India, such as Ebrahim Alkazi, B. V. Karanth, Alyque Padamsee, Prasanna, Amal Allana, Vijaya Mehta, Satyadev Dubey, and Mohit Takalkar. He has also been active as an actor, director, and scriptwriter in Hindi, Marathi, and Kannada films and teleserials. He has acted for film-makers such as Shyam Benegal, Satyajit Ray, Mrinal Sen, Nagesh Kukunoor, and Kabir Khan.

Vanraj Bhatia has composed a full-scale opera based on *The Fire and the Rain*, the first of its kind in India.

The International Theatre Institute of UNESCO, Paris, has declared Karnad a 'World Theatre Ambassador'.

He has been awarded the D.Litt by Karnatak University, Dharwad, Vidyasagar University, Midnapore, and Ravenshaw University, Cuttack, as well as the Honorary D.Litt of the University of Southern California, Los Angeles.

He has been conferred the Padma Bhushan by the President of India, has received the Bharatiya Jnanpith, the country's highest literary award, and has been conferred the Sahitya Akademi award.